LEARNING THROUGH EXPERIENCE

Troubling Orthodoxies and Intersecting Questions

The Professional Practices in Adult Education and Lifelong Learning Series explores issues and concerns of practitioners who work in the broad range of settings in adult and continuing education and lifelong learning.

The books provide information and strategies on how to make practice more effective for professionals and those they serve. They are written from a practical viewpoint and provide a forum for instructors, administrators, policy makers, counselors, trainers, instructional designers, and other related professionals. The series contains single author or coauthored books only and does not include edited volumes.

Sharan B. Merriam
Ronald M. Cervero
Series Editors

LEARNING THROUGH EXPERIENCE

Troubling Orthodoxies and Intersecting Questions

Tara J. Fenwick

KRIEGER PUBLISHING COMPANY
MALABAR, FLORIDA
2003

Original Edition 2003

Printed and Published by
KRIEGER PUBLISHING COMPANY
KRIEGER DRIVE
MALABAR, FLORIDA 32950

Library of Congress Cataloging-in-Publication Data

Fenwick, Tara J.
      Learning through experience : troubling orthodoxies and intersecting questions / Tara J. Fenwick. — Original ed.
            p.   cm. — (The professional practices in adult education and
      lifelong learning series)
      Includes bibliographical references (p.) and index.
      ISBN 1-57524-196-X (alk. paper)
      1. Adult education. 2. Experiential learning. I. Title. II. Series.
      LC5219.F46 2003
      374—dc21   2003040128

10   9   8   7   6   5   4   3   2

CONTENTS

PREFACE

This book is chiefly for newcomers to the field of adult
education in general and adult learning through experience in
particular. My intention has been to bring together, in one overview, writers in various disciplines who contribute to a multifaceted understanding of experiential learning. This overview
both acknowledges theories that have been discussed for many
years and are readily available elsewhere, and provides elementary explanations for contemporary theories that may be less
well known. The point is to introduce readers to authors that I
have found provocative in my own journey of learning and questioning. I do not pretend to offer here a comprehensive review
but a personal exploration of writings that I believe have much
to teach. Notions of experiential learning that I encountered
when first learning the art of practicing adult education contain
certain orthodoxies that some have challenged—but that deserve to be further unsettled. My hope is that where readers find
themselves nodding in agreement or scratching their heads over
particular concepts here, they will be enticed to seek out the rich
sources and their original authors who are cited throughout.

The book is underpinned by five perspectives of learning
that I submit are sufficiently distinct and fecund as to deserve
exploration through various dimensions of adult education. The
book has been organized according to these dimensions. Thus,
after an introductory chapter and an overview of these five perspectives, I examine their contributions to critiques and debates,
suggested roles for adult educators, approaches to educational
practice, and recent research in the field of experiential learning.
While this organization allows for comparison and integration
of these perspectives, it does create some overlap as we cycle

through the perspectives in different domains. However, I happen to believe that an iterative approach may be helpful for those encountering these perspectives for the first time. To accommodate the focus of this series on practical suggestions, rather more emphasis is granted here to pedagogical strategy than may be acceptable to readers sensitive to the technologizing of human learning processes.

Most discussion here is limited to issues of experience raised directly by educational writers, or by learning theorists associated with the field of adult education. What we must keep reminding ourselves is that large areas of philosophical deliberation on experience are often lightly treated or utterly ignored in this literature. So for example, there is still much to learn about experiential learning from myriad authors and practices exploring aesthetic, moral, spiritual, sexual, virtual, indigenous, and hybrid experiences and knowings. Similarly when we as educators invite learners to share narratives of personal experiences, or to critically reflect on their own and others' experiences as an approach to studying learning and development, entire realms of physical, political or intimate experiences are bracketed out by cultural norms, linguistic limitations and social stratifications. I am unsure what messages we convey when we do not acknowledge these dynamics and omissions, or when we treat these narratives as unproblematic representations of memoried experience. I am also troubled by what appears to be, in stories and prescriptions of adult education practice, a certain continuing reliance on "western" reflection-oriented notions of experiential learning, and continuing representations of the educator's presence in experiential learning as almost naturally legitimate, even essential. Alternative perspectives of learning are surprisingly mute, particularly in North American-based adult education literature.

So, in this volume I set out to trouble or disturb some orthodoxies, an endeavor that itself soon proves to be troubling in various conceptual, moral, and practical directions. Part of what becomes troubling is that the questions I ask, rooted in different perspectives, intersect with one another's premises in ways that seem either incommensurable or annihilatory. Furthermore, the questions begin intersecting together such that they fold back on one another, opening fundamental issues about the nature of life, consciousness, and knowledge. All of this is to explain why I prevailed upon the editor to allow me to append, to the self-confidently simple title *Learning through Experience*, the more self-conscious and obscure subtitle, *Troubling Orthodoxies and Intersecting Questions* (with apologies to Kevin Kumashiro, whose title *Troubling Intersections* was provocative for me).

All of learning is experience-based and at some point the distinction of experience and non-experience becomes absurd. Similarly, the distinction between formal and informal learning—learning conducted inside or outside of institutions—assigns undeserved privilege of recognition to classroom contexts, among all the spaces and movements where learning bubbles interminably. Perhaps as adult educators we are too closely invested in the learning enterprise to appreciate its wide-ranging complexity. Perhaps we sometimes leap too quickly to grand purposes, calling one another to visions ranging from social transformation to human growth. I suggest that we might pause again and consider the vast dimensions in a moment of learning through experience, from as many perspectives as we can find, with the humble recognition of our own vast limitations in considering these. This book is offered in this humility of spirit.

ACKNOWLEDGMENTS

I am indebted to Ron Cervero, Sharan Merriam, and Mary Roberts for their editorial work on this book. Thanks also are due to Susan Imel, who first suggested that I develop these ideas on experiential learning into a full-length manuscript, and Arthur (Butch) Wilson, John Dirkx, and Richard Edwards for their general encouragement. Finally, I wish to express sincere thanks to those who contributed to this book through their reviews of earlier iterations of these ideas, in particular: Sandra Kerka, Edward Taylor, Verna Willis, David Stein, and Jilian W. Fewell. All errors are my own.

THE AUTHOR

Tara J. Fenwick is an assistant professor of adult education in the Department of Educational Policy Studies at the University of Alberta in Edmonton, Alberta, Canada. Her research and teaching focus on learning through work; in particular, the nature of experiential learning in changing contexts of work such as contingent employment and self-employment. She has published articles in the *International Journal of Lifelong Education, Studies in the Education of Adults, Studies in Continuing Education, Work, Employment and Society* and the *Adult Education Quarterly* critically examining experiential learning, worker development, negotiation of identities in work, innovative learning, women's learning in work, complex systems of work learning, and the nature of desire in work-related learning. She has served as cochair of the Canadian Commission of Professors of Adult Education, the vice-president of the Canadian Association for the Study of Adult Education, and the book review editor for the *Adult Education Quarterly*. She has been adjunct or visiting faculty member at the University of Calgary, the University of Nova Scotia, Mount St. Vincent University, St. Stephen's Theological College, and St. Francis Xavier University. Her previously published books included *Work and Leisure* (1994) and *The Art of Evaluation: A Handbook for Educators and Trainers* (coauthored with Jim Parsons, 2000, Thompson Educational Publishers). For her work she was awarded the Coutts-Clarke Research Fellowship at the University of Alberta, and the Alberta Book of the Year award with her coauthor Jim Parsons.

CHAPTER 1

Why a Book about Experiential Learning? Introduction and Background

"A fresh hope is astir. From many quarters the call to a new kind of education with its initial assumption affirming that education is life . . . The whole of life is learning, therefore education can have no endings."

These words were published in 1926 by a man who started his career as a laborer, entered agricultural extension work, and eventually became a professor and writer deeply dedicated to promoting adult learning through experience in everyday life: his name was Eduard Lindeman. Today experiential learning is, as Elana Michelson (1996) suggests, arguably one of the most significant areas for current research and practice in adult education. The term *experiential learning* is often used both to distinguish the flow of ongoing meaning-making in our lives from theoretical knowledge and to distinguish nondirected "informal" life experience from "formal" education. Much adult learning is commonly understood to be located in everyday workplace tasks and interactions, home and family activity, community involvement, and other important sites of nonformal and sometimes unacknowledged education. Many of us believe that our skills and concepts, and certainly the development of our practical knowledge, the know-how that we use in our daily activities and work, are best learned through "doing." This belief has led to a body of research and practice in adult education directed at questions like these, which will be examined in this book:

- How do people actually learn from their experiences?
- What are the most significant kinds of experience for different knowledges?
- What is the relationship between learning and doing, and between learner and context?
- What is the nature and role of consciousness?
- Is the nature of experiential knowing different from knowledge developed through formal education?
- Under what circumstances does knowledge developed through experience transfer to other situations?

But wait—just what are we talking about when we refer to experience that becomes part of a learning process? Some educational literature focuses on immediate concrete experience, showing how to involve people in and help them learn from activities that engage them physically, emotionally, sensually, and relationally (i.e., Richards, 1992). So, are we to exclude experiences commonly associated with more traditional formal education, such as reading, listening, discussing, writing, and thinking? Other literature understands experience as people's biographies, showing how to help individuals learn through recalling, analysing, reframing, and articulating their life histories (i.e., Dominicé, 2000). But if we include all human experience, then is not every minute of our lives, and every part of our ongoing sense-making, actually experiential learning? Writers such as Anita Malinen (2000) have grappled with the question of where to place the boundaries around experiential learning in adult education.

Fundamental to all of these issues is an essential question: what do we mean by learning? As we will see in Chapter 2, there are many answers to this, often contradicting one another. Dialogues are currently unfolding about how this learning takes place. Some, like Michelson (1996, 1999), have criticized the common understanding of reflection-on-experience that still dominates much educational theory and practice of experiential learning today. According to this notion, people supposedly

construct mental knowledge structures by recalling and analysing lived experience. Michelson and many others introduced in
Chapter 2 suggest that this understanding creates an unnatural
split between thinking and action (as well as between mind/
body and individual/context). Implicit in this reflection-on-
experience notion is a process of privatizing, objectifying, or-
dering, and disciplining fluid human experience. This reflective
orientation also often ignores issues of identity, politics, and the
ways human experience is actually produced through particular
cultural images and language. Others such as Jean Lave and
Etienne Wenger (1991) and Dennis Sumara and Brent Davis
(1997) propose conceptions of experiential learning that focus
on socio-cultural dynamics, trajectories of action, and complexities of context rather than the mental activity of a person learning. Still others probe the ways we resist, even hate, learning
certain threatening or difficult knowledge, and are driven by our
attraction to obtain or imitate other knowledge through learning (Britzman, 1998a). These perspectives and concerns are described in more detail in Chapters 2 and 4.

Perhaps most immediately important for practitioners are
questions about the role of the educator, and the appropriate
place and form of intentionally designed occasions for experiential learning. In the world of adult education the notion of
experiential learning has been appropriated to designate everything from kinesthetic directed instructional activities in the
classroom, to special workplace projects interspersed with critical dialogue led by a facilitator, to learning generated through
social action movements, to the deep reflection involved in autobiographical writing, and even to team-building adventures in
the wilderness. Chapter 5 explores some of these roles in terms
of their assumptions and allegiances.

We must not forget that experiential learning became popular in adult education to celebrate and legitimate people's experience as significant in their knowledge development. As one
way to resist the authority of technical disciplinary knowledge,
it acknowledged the *process* of learning as much as the *outcome*
in terms of new skills and concepts developed. Adult educators were also motivated by a genuine desire to counter a gen-

eral lack of recognition or reward for experience in workplaces and higher education because experiential knowing has been traditionally uncredentialed. Their pedagogy, when focused on learners' experience, challenged well-established ways of thinking about education as program, the educator as expert knower, and knowledge as theory. In practice, experiential learning in adult education has included the following activities:

1. Field-based experience or off-site learning, such as internships, service learning, or apprenticeships.

2. Credit for prior learning, where an adult seeking entrance to a postsecondary program submits evidence of learning through work experience and life experience to be assessed for advance credit (variously called RPL, APEL, or PLA, Prior Learning Assessment).

3. Classroom-based active learning exercises where instruction is embedded in hands-on activities in which learners participate, then reflect and discuss their learnings.

4. Outdoor education programs designed to develop leadership, problem-solving, self-awareness or team skills. Sometimes these programs are offered in corporate training to help people develop more creativity, risk-taking, and communication skills by recognizing the barriers to their own potential and productivity.

5. Learning through ongoing everyday meaning-making. Sometimes in research studies this sort of experiential learning is called practical intelligence. Sometimes it is referred to as informal learning (in contrast to formal learning which tends to signify institutional schooling). Several studies have examined the development of professional expertise through ongoing everyday experiential learning.

6. Learning through social action. This approach understands experiential learning to be enmeshed in the activity of a community. Two examples are described based on different purposes of learning. The first is the experiential learning by which individuals become active, competent participants

within the joint action and culture of the community. The second is when the collective resists some dominant or oppressive force through social action, the experience of which can transform the group and its members.

Experiential educators have developed a multitude of strategies and activities connected with each of these approaches. Selections are presented in Chapter 6. However, critics argue there has been a shift, that experiential learning is itself becoming institutionalized and regulated. Wilma Fraser (1995), in reflecting on her 20 years working with adult experiential education in the United Kingdom, laments the turn to assessing adults' experience for institutional uses. She and other writers appearing in this book have raised concern about this incorporation of experience, arguing that the highly idiosyncratic nature of experience among different individuals, in different situations, at different times of their lives, cannot and should not be packaged and regulated as some form of education.

So beyond the "what" and "how" questions that educators ask about experiential learning, are important ethical questions about "why" and "should," leading us to examine our purposes. As Peter Alheit (1998) has pointed out, the appropriation of human life experience as a pedagogical project to be managed by educators is highly suspicious. Perhaps, wonder some critics, the educator's motivation to interfere with individuals' experience is a colonizing impulse. When educators try to capture, measure, judge, and wring learning from fluid spaces of human life and meaning-making, they exploit experience as a sort of calculable resource to serve rationalistic and utilitarian notions of knowledge. In a time when an understanding of managed experiential learning is ascending as a primary animator of lifelong learning, there is an urgent need to disrupt and resist reductionist, individualized notions of experiential learning and pose alternative conceptions.

This need has motivated this book. Theories of learning continue to multiply, and within this vast and fascinating field there have emerged alternative perspectives that present particularly exciting challenges to dominant notions of experiential learning. These learning perspectives come from unexpected fields and are in varying stages of development, ranging from evolutionary biology and mathematics to cultural anthropology, cultural geography, feminism, and critical discourse studies. Some perspectives, like psychoanalysis, have been recovered and reworked from older schools of thought in learning. These wide-ranging explanations of how learning happens are each grounded in and propelled by different purposes. For educators, the possibilities for conceptualizing learning and clarifying pedagogical purposes presented by these perspectives may help overcome certain limitations and undesirable consequences associated with experiential learning practice. Meanwhile these perspectives may help reinforce and enrich experiential learning traditions that have flowered in fruitful directions for adult education. Before turning to these perspectives in Chapter 2, the remaining sections provide a short overview of the history and dimensions of experiential learning in North American adult education.

A BRIEF TOUR OF EXPERIENTIAL LEARNING IN ADULT EDUCATION

Adult education has a long tradition of honoring experiential learning. Apprenticeship training for trades and professions is based on beliefs that important learning is rooted in repeated practice of skills in different situations, using actual tools (including language) in real contexts, while coping with the social and political dynamics important to any working community. In other words, people learn through complex elements of experience that cannot be duplicated in a classroom. Progressive educator John Dewey, in his classic little book *Experience and Education* first published in 1938, challenged the reigning pedagogy and justified education based on learning by doing. He showed how individuals create new knowledge and transform themselves through a process of learning by performing new roles. Dewey was interested in education for a democracy, the social nature of learning, and internal growth and process. He

emphasized that not all experience educates. We have all wit-
nessed or lived through episodes from which people can emerge
apparently unchanged, not having learned lessons that others
have attended to in the same experience. As well, sometimes we
learn things from our experience that are actually harmful to
our own or others' growth or well-being. Dewey wrote that for
learning to happen, an experience must include two key dimensions. First is *continuity*: the learner needs to be able to connect
aspects of the new experience to what he or she already knows,
in ways that modify this knowledge. The second is *interaction*:
the learner needs to be actively interacting with his or her environment, testing out lessons developed in that environment.
Dewey believed the educator should help link disparate experiences into a coherent whole. His ideas about progressive learning influenced decades of educational thought, both in public
K-12 curriculum development and in adult education.

A friend and colleague of Dewey's, Eduard Lindeman
(1926), also was committed to social justice achieved through
learning in action. For Lindeman, four beliefs above all must
drive adult education: (1) that learning is everyday experience;
(2) that learning is driven by nonvocational ideals, specifically,
putting meaning into the whole of life; (3) that learning must
be based on actual situations in adults' experience; and (4) that
the learners' experience is the resource of highest value. Lindeman's "situation-approach" was an early articulation of the in-
separability of learning and doing:

> Small groups of aspiring adults who desire to keep their minds
> fresh and vigorous; who begin to learn by confronting pertinent
> situations; who dig down into the reservoirs of their experience
> before resorting to texts and secondary facts; who are led in the
> discussion by teachers who are also searchers after wisdom and
> not oracles; this constitutes the setting for adult education, the
> modern quest for life's meaning. (Lindeman, 1926, p. 7)

It is evident that social action and community development
have maintained strong relationships with the field of experiential learning. Moses Coady and Jimmy Tompkins animated the
Antigonish Movement in Nova Scotia in the 1920s on prin-

ciples of adults learning through the experience of action to improve their economic quality of life, creating what they needed through small groups. Civil activism such as Myles Horton's (1990) work at Tennessee's Highlander Center during the 1950s and 60s was committed to learning through social action: small groups decided the issues of their oppression, then together learned the necessary resources (including liberating their own creativity) to take action towards resolving these issues. More recently, Michael Newman (1999), Griff Foley (1999), and Tom Heaney (1996) have shown how and what people learn informally through such political action. Activities such as popular theatre (Prentki & Selman, 2000) and community story-telling (Von Kotz, 2000) also have long traditions in community-based experiential learning initiatives, as ways of involving people actively in collective analysis of their experience towards taking action to improve their lives.

In the 1960s and 70s with the rise of humanistic psychology, experiential learning with its emphasis on placing the learner at the heart of the learning process began to acquire status as a movement. Malcolm Knowles (1970) in particular focused North American adult educators' attention on the importance of experience as one of the five principles of his theory of andragogy or adult learning. Knowles argued for a learner-centered educational process, where adult learners are encouraged to reflect upon and share their biographies of experience rather than simply accept the authority of texts (content) foreign to their own experiences. Knowles's ideas are responsible for a sweeping wave of change in the 1970s, where lecturers became facilitators of dialogue, and learners exercised voice in determining the issues, goals, and applications of course materials.

The importance of reflection in experiential learning has been developed extensively by David Kolb (1984), whose model suggested how reflection and action are related in experiential learning; Jack Mezirow (1990, 1991, 1996), who showed how people undergo perspective transformation through critical reflection on their experience; and Paulo Freire (1970), whose theory of conscientization and praxis—learning through radical action combined with critical reflection—has galvanized emancipatory education around the world. Donald Schön (1983, 1987) popularized an approach to professional education he called reflection-in-action which acknowledged that important learning unfolds through problem solving in the heat of every-day messy experience, where problems are ill-structured, outcomes uncertain, and situational dimensions constantly shifting.

David Boud and his associates (1991, 1993) have also written extensively on experiential learning in adult education. They maintain, as do others, that learners must be (consciously) engaged for learning to occur at any level. Like Kolb, Knowles, Mezirow, and Freire, Boud and Walker (1991) assume that our construction of learning from experience is an intentional act: as learners we are always actively pursuing knowledge and will find opportunities for learning in a variety of situations, whether labeled educative or not. Theories of informal learning, such as the model presented by Victoria Marsick and Karen Watkins (1992), showed how adults often learn to understand puzzling new situations, or develop new skills, without going near a classroom. They suggested that while informal learning is planned and intentional (though controlled by the learner), incidental learning occurs almost unconsciously, such as when we start a new job and before long, find out we have somehow absorbed important cultural knowledge about the politics and norms of the organization. Some writers describe this continuous active pursuit of knowledge as ongoing meaning-making. A movement in using life history and autobiography for pedagogical purposes has argued that an important need for many adults in a postmodern time of fragmentation and anxiety is to find coherence in their experiences and celebrate their ongoing meaning-making (i.e., West, 1996).

Throughout its history, educational interest in experiential learning has typically championed recognition and valuing of the learner's personal practical knowledge and informal or incidental experience, to resist domination by disciplinary bodies of theoretical and canonical knowledge. This is why experiential learning was often understood to be radical, associated with learner empowerment, and sometimes evangelistic in tone. As Fiona Reeve and Jim Gallacher (1999) argue, "taking experience as the starting point for learning has the potential at least to erode traditional boundaries between knowledge and skills, vocational and academic learning, and between disciplines" (p. 127). Much of the focus on experiential learning throughout the twentieth century has intended to challenge prevailing ortho- doxy that worthwhile or legitimate education is planned and properly accredited, and occurs only in programs, institutions, and classrooms. For some, learner empowerment has meant transformation through recognizing the power of one's own (in- formal) experience, and naming the oppressions one has suf- fered, as a step towards personal emancipation and possibly tak- ing action for change.

However, others argue that experiential learning is itself developing its own orthodoxies such as Assessment of Prior Ex- periential Learning. As Colin Griffin (1992) claims,

> We are witnessing the transformation of experiential learning from a progressive educational movement towards reconstruc- tion as an object of institutional policy and professional good practice. As such, it is being incorporated or absorbed into the formal system of educational provision. (p. 31)

In terms of adult education in the area of experiential learn- ing, Susan Warner Weil and Ian McGill (1989) distinguish four different forms of educational practice that they call "villages":

Village 1. Accrediting learning derived from experience for purpose of entry to educational progression or em- ployment. This is variously called Assessment of Prior Experience and Learning, Prior Learning Assessment (PLA), or Recognition of Prior Learning (RPL). For edu- cators gathered in this village, reflection is about record- ing and assessing experience. The first model was the U.S. GI Bill of 1946 which dealt with returning World War II veterans who wanted their experience credited to enter university, so it was assessed using traditional uni- versity course materials.

Village 2. Using experiential learning to challenge higher education and continuing education schools and curricu-

lum. Deriving from the progressive tradition of Dewey and Lindeman, educators help learners unveil their hidden untapped knowledge through reflection on life experience.

Village 3. Focus on social change. In this radical tradition, educators help learners see outside their private world of reflection, and become aware of the broader sociocultural dynamics and history shaping both their life experience and their ways of reflecting on it.

Village 4. Focus on individual development. From a humanist perspective, educators in this village encourage personal growth and individuals taking responsibility for their own self-learning.

As we can see, the organizing principle governing the division of practice into these villages is the purpose of the educator in terms of desired outcomes for the learner. The villages do not distinguish between ways of actually conceptualizing experience and the process of cognition or learning entangled within it. Tony Saddington (1998) took Weil and McGill's widely referenced four villages one step further: he showed that while the villages categorize experiential learning according to educators' immediate *purposes*, activities within each village reflect three fundamentally different orientations to education and learning. These orientations are *progressive*, focusing on the individuals' responsibility towards their society, and viewing education as a problem-solving instrument of social and political reform; *humanist*, focusing on the learner at the center of a process of discovery and self-actualization, in a drive towards personal enrichment, integration, and psychological development; and *radical*, focusing on societal and individual liberation through questioning and reinterpreting the very cultural assumptions of experience, and moving to action for transformation. However, all three of these orientations and all four villages presume the same basic conceptualization of experiential learning: an independent learner, cognitively reflecting on concrete experience to construct new understandings, perhaps with the assistance of an educator, towards some social goal of progress or improvement. As we will see in Chapter 2, this is only one of many conceptions of the actual process of experiential learning. These conceptions begin by asking questions about the nature of human experience and itself, and often come to different conclusions. In an attempt to reconcile various positions and search for the "essences" of adult experiential learning, Anita Malinen (2000) presents a comparison of the theories of Malcolm Knowles, David Kolb, Jack Mezirow, Reg Revans, and Donald Schön. She states:

> Adult experiential learning is a complex, vague and ambiguous phenomenon, which is still inadequately defined, conceptually suspect—and even poorly researched . . . on the other hand, its theoretical and philosophical foundations are fragmented and confusing . . . There are too many interpretations and priorities among the theorists and practitioners that no single, clear definition of these foundations could be constructed. (p. 15)

A useful starting point might be exploring our own beliefs about just what constitutes experience. The next section introduces issues to ponder in five dimensions of human experience. What is the individual's purpose? What are the various ways of interpreting and engaging in the experience? How do these different ways influence what is learned? What is the relationship of the experiencing individual's self to the context of the experience? How can we understand the experience and learning that are somehow processed through this relationship?

THINKING ABOUT THE NATURE
OF EXPERIENCE

Various writers addressing experiential learning have pointed out that everyday human experiences vary dramatically in kind. We have routine and nonroutine experiences, related to activities as different as everyday problem solving, critical turning points in life, adjustments to unfamiliar contexts, and learning in and about relationships. Experience comes in different dimensions. Of course there is *direct embodied experience*: an immediate encounter in the here-and-now, planned or unplanned, involving us physically, emotionally, sensually, mentally, and perhaps spiritually. But we also can learn from *vicarious experience*, listening to or reading about the experience of others and imagining ourselves immersed in the encounter. We sometimes are exposed to *simulated experience*, a direct experience planned to be like something real, but controlled within an artificial context. We can experience through *reliving* a past encounter through our memories, sometimes experiencing the event differently because we bring a new perspective about ourselves, the situation, or its meaning in context of later events. Furthermore, reliving through introspection is a different experience than reliving through dialogue, for performing a story and incorporating spectator response is quite different than mentally circling through our own scripts and meanings. Michael Newman (1999) adds to *experience recalled* a form that he calls *experience forgotten*, that long-buried memory which may unexpectedly surface in sudden and powerful remembrance to redirect our learning. There is also *collaborative experience*, joining others in a shared community of experience whose meaning is constructed together amid conversation and joint action. But experience does not necessarily demand physical participation: *introspective experience*, such as meditation or dreaming, or reading, are powerful forms of experience occurring in a special psychic space where our awareness of physical being, time, and geographic location are often suspended from our consciousness. All of these dimensions suggest different ways to understand whatever is construed to be learning in each context.

Purpose

An important dimension of how we experience, especially in terms of learning, is our purpose. We can approach the same situation with an intention of accomplishing a task (such as solving a problem, building a relationship, or causing something to change), learning something new, gaining pleasure or entertainment, resting and refreshing—or some combination of these. Our approach will affect what we learn. For example, we are often faced with computer glitches that must be solved before we can proceed in our work. We may ask a colleague for some quick help, watching over her shoulder as she quickly executes the commands needed to fix the problem, and possibly learning a little about the procedure. We may also learn, as we observe, something about our colleague's process of working, about her relationship with us, about our own impatience, and so on. We might approach the experience differently if we wanted to learn how to fix the problem for ourselves in the future, or how to understand the logic of fixing computer problems. Perhaps we would write down the steps as we observed, asking questions to clarify, then practicing them ourselves. We certainly would observe with more focus and engagement. However, we may experience different degrees of consciousness about our intentions to learn (Eraut, 2000). These may range from fully aware and intentional deliberative learning to spontaneous reactive learning where we are aware but surprised by the learning moment, to totally implicit learning without intention or awareness (Eraut, 2000). Another way of viewing our learning purposes, posed by psychoanalytic theorists, is that ongoing psychic activity in our unconscious repulses or attracts us to particular knowledge. We are thus never innocently unaware or ignorant of our learning, but are actively pushing away conscious knowledge. Wilfred Bion (1994) highlights the implicit difficulty in learning from experience—forcing us to tolerate frustration and uncertainty, to reconsider the meanings of our past experiences, and to change our relationship to our past knowledge—as producing our unconscious hatred of development. This essential hatred or resistance to learning opens interesting questions not only about our own and others' multilayered learning experiences, but also about educators' insistence that development is inherently a good thing.

In educational understandings of experiential learning, the purposes of the person doing the experiencing may come into conflict with others' purposes, represented by the curriculum, the cultural norms that accept certain views of what counts as an experience and ignore others, and the instructor's and peers' purposes. Any educator intervening in experiential learning does so presumptuously, and therefore should be ethically obligated to declare clear purposes for doing so that can be critically scrutinized by learners and others affected by pedagogical actions.

Interpretation

How we interpret an experience will also affect how we recall it, and thus what we learn from it. For example, imagine someone who is giving a presentation at work about a difficult project, and receiving strong critical reaction from coworkers. This someone might engage the experience as a struggle to be survived, a failure to be forgotten, or a valuable learning experience to be applied. In terms of emotion, some may engage the experience as humiliating and disappointing, others as an interesting challenge. In context of other priorities, some may view it as productive, towards a valued purpose, others as wasted time.

Our interpretation is mediated by the concepts and language we bring to an experience. We actually *produce* our experiences because, among all the complex and contradictory dimensions in a given event, we are highly selective in what we notice and highlight. We make associations based on what we have already seen. We explain things in terms of theories we already hold, our cultural aesthetic notions of what is beautiful or ugly, and our socialized morality judging things as good or bad. We usually don't notice what we don't understand, or we try to impose upon it the vocabularies we have already learned, which often distorts what we encounter. Consider 19th century British descriptions of Africa: typically these were exoticized and alienating, reflecting the writers' struggle to reconcile their European concepts and language with phenomena that did not fit.

Engagement

We engage different experiences with a range of positions, processes, and intensity. We may plunge in actively, or observe. For example, the extent of our sense of responsibility in a situation, for ourselves and others, often determines our level of participation. Our positionality in any situation may be affected by our sense of competence and familiarity, of authority and power relative to others, and of caring about what happens. Sometimes we participate only peripherally in a community because we are not allowed a voice by others. Our desire is always located in a particular way in any situation, which shapes the way we attend to what is around us and experience these dimensions. For example in a classroom experiential game, a learner may desire most to be recognized as competent, to be liked by the instructor, to be stimulated by fresh ideas, to be noticed by others, to not be noticed by others, to laugh and have fun, to win the game, to master a new procedure, and so on. The direction of our desire influences the mode of participation, and the extent to which our desires are fulfilled slants the way the experience is interpreted.

Self

To understand experiential learning we must probe the relation between self and society. In conventional orientations to experiential learning, the assumption often is that humans exist as individual selves that naturally develop towards greater maturity, expansiveness, consolidation and sense of worth, fulfillment, and integration. This unitary self philosophy, so pervasive in the humanistic psychology movement affecting many current

conceptions of adult education, arose through the past two cen-
turies of privatizing and psychologizing the "inner space." As
Elana Michelson (1999) shows, the enlightenment period inaugurated an era of Western obsession with the human individual
self and its identity. However, many writers in the past few decades have seriously challenged this notion. Some, from a feminist orientation, observe that the self is not single and solitary,
but woven into different relational networks. We in fact have
multiple selves that emerge and shift according to circumstance
(Clark & Dirkx, 2000), and find positions in various communities. Others (Bracher, 1993; Britzman, 1998a; Ellsworth,
1997) draw attention to the significance of our unmapped unconscious in our experiences. This other conscious acts out desires and expresses characteristics of our selves that we often
conveniently ignore or repress in our conscious reflection about
who we are.

Still others from a poststructural orientation (such as Foucault, 1980, 1988) use the term *subject*, maintaining that what
we think of as the self in fact is produced in a web of social
practices and language. The subject has no existence per se, but
is brought into presence according to the actions we observe
ourselves engaging, and the stories we use to name a continuous
concrete self at the center of these actions. This has been described as a postmodern, de-centered view of the self:

> subjectivity without a centre of origin, caught in meanings, po-
> sitioned in the language and narratives of the culture. The self
> cannot know itself independently of the significations in which
> it is enmeshed. . . . Meanings are always in play and the self,
> caught up in this play, is an ever changing self. (Usher, Bryant &
> Johnson, 1997, p. 103)

Mimi Orner (1992) explains that the switch from conceptions of self to subjects encourages us to "think of ourselves and
our realities as constructions; the products of meaning-making
activity which are both culturally specific and generally unconscious" (p. 79). Our subjectivity, who we are and how we think
about who we are, emerges through our engagement within the

practices, discourses, moralities, and institutions that give significance to events in our worlds. We are not even conscious of the various selves we inhabit in everyday experience.

Context

The contexts within which we move also shape the nature of our experience. Context includes historical location and meanings of an activity, its geographical space and movement, as well as its cultural meanings and socio-political dynamics. Various regulations, formal and informal, determine what can and cannot be thought or expressed. Powerful ideas produce our beliefs about what action is desirable, what is significant, what is taboo or invisible, and what experience means. David Beckett and Paul Hager (2000) suggest that educators attend to four key dimensions of context in workplace learning, which could apply to many other situations of adult urban experiential learning in the 21st century: pervasive change and crisis, recognition of difference and diversity, focus on the particular and local, and recognition of political and social dimensions of knowledge (p. 145). They also point out that dynamic elements of context are interrelated in complex ways. A situation is characterized by a specific combination of features at any given time, and it changes over time. Individuals' responses to a situation are also unpredictable, and shaped by social forces and personal dispositions (attitudes, values, and beliefs). Richard Edwards and Robin Usher (2000) show that people's sense of location has been disturbed and dispersed through contemporary forces (new patterns of urbanization, information technologies, flexible employment, and community ruptures). Our postmodern sense of dislocation may cause anxiety, but also offers new possibilities. In any context we may take up different locations or identities. We may experience different contexts simultaneously, as when we participate in a listserve discussion while sitting in our family home.

Many writers emphasize that people cannot be understood as separated from their contexts. We are enmeshed with our cultures, and the communities of activity within which we act and make choices. These change constantly, and we accordingly adapt, resist, initiate opportunity, or are swept along in the routines structuring our actions. We may think of our own experiences as natural and real, and ourselves as rational interpreters learning new ideas through these experiences. But cultural theorists show that we view and feel what happens through the values and norms of our culture. In our perceptions we emphasize those actions, people, and events that are culturally important, that carry status in the communities with which we affiliate ourselves. Our cultural communities judge certain phenomena as normal and others as deviant or problematic. So cultural theorists say our experiences, and in fact we ourselves, are actually *constructed* within particular cultural discourses. These usually favor a dominant group, its symbols of power, its ideal images, its notions of what count as important things to know and what is invisible or frivolous, and its desired order of things.

Here is where the dimension of power and its link to knowledge, language, and identity becomes critical in understanding learning in experience. Here is also where we must seriously consider our entanglements with our cultural contexts before we assume, unproblematically, that we simply enter an experience, reflect upon it to make meaning, then apply its lessons in a process we like to think of as learning.

These five dimensions entangled in experience and learning -purpose, interpretation, engagement, self, and context—continue to be questioned throughout this book. Chapter 2 offers a comparative summary of perspectives on experiential learning. It begins with the reflective constructivist view of experiential learning, then presents four very different theoretical orientations that have emerged in recent scholarly writing addressing (experiential) learning and cognition. Chapter 3 returns to key questions about experiential learning, touched upon briefly at the beginning of this chapter, that have been raised by adult educators. We hear responses to these questions offered from the different perspectives about experiential learning, as well as their challenges to each other's responses. In Chapter 4, criticisms and debates about experiential learning introduced in the preceding paragraphs are developed in further detail, along with recommendations and cautions for educators generated through these debates.

For readers most interested in recommendations for educational practice, Chapter 5 describes roles for educators suggested by different perspectives and Chapter 6 offers a selection of strategies and activities aligned with different perspectives of experiential learning. Finally, it seemed appropriate for a book exploring dilemmas raised by many perspectives to close with questions rather than answers, so Chapter 7 presents the most recent issues emerging in theory and practice related to experiential learning. Readers are offered suggestions for making sense of their own practice and beliefs amidst all of these debates and conflicting perspectives. Hopefully we all can resist the urge to ignore these unsettling issues and seize techniques for answers to practice. Let us instead dwell in—even relish—the questions as being practice itself. The writing of this book has been driven by three questions in particular: What is the nature of the intersection between individual(s), situation, social relationships, and knowing? Is there a legitimate role for an educator in this process? Where educators have an ethical role to play in experiential learning, what purposes and approaches should guide this role? Let us turn next to what other theorists, with dramatically different philosophies of life and learning, have to say about these questions.

CHAPTER 2

What Is the Theoretical Base? Different Conceptions of Experiential Learning

This chapter compares the premises, focuses, and orientations to education of five different perspectives on experiential learning. First presented is the dominant constructivist conception of experiential learning, based on a belief that individuals construct personal knowledge by mentally *reflecting on concrete experience*. Then four alternative conceptions of experiential learning challenging constructivism will be introduced. These represent distinct currents of thought, not just single authors' theories, which have emerged in recent scholarly writing addressing (experiential) learning and cognition. They were selected either because of their prominence in recent writing about learning and development, or because they offer an original perspective on the relationships among experience, context, mind, and learning that present interesting challenges to the dominant constructivist view. The first alternative conceptualizes learning as *participating in a community of practice*, based on a situative theory of learning. In contrast to constructivism, this perspective believes knowledge is not developed in individuals' minds through reflection, but in groups through their interactions. The next perspective focuses upon *attuning to unconscious desires and fears*, based on psychoanalytic theories that are enjoying an energetic renaissance and reformulation in contemporary writing about teaching and learning, which as yet have not become prominent in adult education. Another perspective is concerned about *resisting dominant norms of experience*. Based on critical theories of pedagogy and culture, this orientation has enjoyed widespread interest, attention and dissemination in adult education literature committed to social justice and human emancipation. Finally, a relatively new perspective concentrates on *exploring ecological relationships between cognition and environment*. Based on complexity theory and systems theory, this view of experiential learning has only recently been incorporated into pedagogical theorizing in North America.

These five perspectives are described briefly in this chapter, outlining each one's view of experiential learning and the role of the educator. These descriptions are intended as an overview only, to help show the contrasts between each position and the key areas where its orientation differs from other explanations of experiential learning. These key areas tend to focus on the following questions: How does learning happen? What is knowledge? How does the learner interact with the thing being learned? How is the learner connected with the context of learning? What is the actual process of experiential learning? What are the purposes and desirable outcomes of experiential learning? How does power influence the learning? Table 2.1, located in the conclusion of this chapter, summarizes the different responses to each of these questions implied by the five perspectives presented below.

REFLECTING UPON CONCRETE EXPERIENCE
(Constructivist Theory of Learning)

The most prevalent understanding of experiential learning is based on reflection on experience. This casts the individual as a central actor in a drama of personal meaning-making. The learner supposedly reflects on concrete lived experience, then interprets and generalizes this experience to form mental structures. These structures are knowledge, stored in memory as concepts that can be represented, expressed, and transferred to new situations. Theoretical models in this perspective explain ways people attend to and perceive experience, interpret and categorize it as concepts, then continue adapting or transforming their conceptual structures. Thus individuals are understood to actively construct their own knowledge, not passively absorb already existing concepts, through interaction with their environments. This school of thought is commonly known as constructivism.

Constructivism has a long and distinguished history, although many different perspectives coexist within it[1] (Piaget, 1966; Von Glaserfeld, 1984; Vygotsky, 1978; Wells, 1995), portraying learners as independent creators and constructors of knowledge, with varying capacity or confidence to rely on their own constructions. However all views share one central premise: a learner is believed to construct, through reflection, a personal understanding of relevant structures of meaning derived from his or her action in the world. In contrast to earlier views, constructivism shifts from the assumption that learning is "taking things in," to a view of learners continuously adapting—in their interpretations and perceptions as well as actions—to the situations around them.

The Swiss psychologist Jean Piaget (1966), after observing children learn through play, described this construction process as oscillating between *assimilation* and *accommodation*. He suggested that learning happens when individuals interact with objects in their environment (which can be material things, names for things, concepts, relationships, etc.) to build and refine constructs of knowledge in their heads. Individuals sometimes assimilate new objects of knowledge by incorporating them into their personal internal network of knowledge constructs. Other times individuals accommodate by altering these constructs when confronting new experiences which may contradict their past knowledge. The important issue is that each individual is active in the learning process, and each person may construct very different understandings after interacting with the same objects in the same environment. This notion challenged ideas of knowledge as a body of information created by scientists and experts, existing outside of individuals.

The Russian Lev Vygotsky (1978) emphasized the role of individuals' interactions with their socio-cultural environment in this process of constructing knowledge. He developed a theory of what he called the "zone of proximal development," a time-bounded site of community activity surrounding a person which can limit or enhance cognitive development. The person learns by engaging fully in this zone, particularly through dialogue. Vygotsky's ideas have been influential in subsequent situative theories of learning.[2] However Vygotsky, like other constructivists, believed that the outcome and objective of learning was the development of individual consciousness, experiencing self-mastery, through a process of reflection (what Vygotsky called "inner speech") as well as interaction with people and objects in the external world.

In adult education, the constructivist view of experiential learning has helped educators focus on the learner, and particularly on learners' active meaning-making processes, challenging the assumption that learners passively absorbed information presented to them. Furthermore, constructivism shows each learner's experiences as unique and highly unpredictable. It understands learning itself as involving the body, mind, emotions, and social relations as individuals experiment with objects and actions in their environments to build knowledge. In adult education, constructivism and the importance of encouraging people to reflect on their experience have tended to dominate understandings of learning. The notion of self-directed learning, first advocated by adult educators such as Malcolm Knowles (1970), understands individual learners intentionally pursuing competence in some area by designing and reflecting upon learning experiences for themselves.

For writers such as David Boud and David Walker (1991), Stephen Brookfield (1995), David Kolb (1984), Jack Mezirow (1991), and Donald Schön (1983), a person's reflection is elevated as the key to unlocking meaning and building knowledge from his or her experience. The individual constructs new knowledge through experimentation, guided by personal intention, selecting focuses for learning from possibilities presented in the environment, and reflectively analysing these experiments. The outcome is personal growth: the individual develops in a progression towards greater maturity and more refined knowledge. For those advocating critical reflection, the outcome of experiential learning is often dramatic change in the individual's view of reality. Specific constructivist models of experiential learning through reflection will be provided in the next chapter. But first we should note that critics of constructivism have complained about its inadequate attention to situational context and social politics, its narrow focus on the individual and the individual's mind, and its splitting of fluid systemic learning into individual parts. The perspectives offered by these critics are briefly presented in the four sections following.

PARTICIPATING IN A COMMUNITY OF PRACTICE
(Situative Theory of Learning)

An alternative view of learning is proposed by situative perspectives (i.e. Brown, Collins & Duguid, 1989; Greeno, 1997; Lave & Wenger, 1991; Rogoff, 1990; Wenger, 1998). These argue that learning is rooted in the situation in which a person participates, not in the head of that person as intellectual concepts produced by reflection. Knowing and learning are defined as engaging in changing processes of social activity. These narratives, relations, and practices are "the property of a kind of community created over time by the sustained pursuit of a shared enterprise . . . communities of practice" (Wenger, 1998, p. 45). Knowledge is not considered a substance to be ingested and then transferred to new situation, but part of the very process of *participation* in the immediate situation and community of practice.

Jean Lave and Etienne Wenger (1991) argue that the understandings that emerge in and help a person to participate in a situation are intimately entwined with the particular community, tools, and activity of that situation. In other words, individuals learn *as* they participate by interacting with the community (with its history, assumptions and cultural values, rules, and patterns of relationship), the tools at hand (including objects, technology, languages, and images), and the moment's activity (its purposes, norms, and practical challenges). Knowledge emerges from these elements interacting. Thus knowing is unendingly inventive and entwined with doing (Lave, 1988). The objective is to become a full participant in the community of practice, not to learn *about* the practice. The community itself defines what constitutes legitimate practice. Newcomers to a community of practice start learning through "legitimate peripheral participation" (Lave & Wenger, 1991); that is, by working at the margins at first, observing, practicing a little, getting to know and interact with a few community members, and thus gradually becoming integrated into the networks of action.

Because knowledge *flows in action*, situative theorists argue strongly that it can be neither commodified as a conceptual substance, nor considered as centered in any way within individual subjects. Stephen Pile and Nigel Thrift (1995) argue that first, understanding is created within conduct itself, which flows ceaselessly, is adaptable but not often deliberately intentional, and is always future-oriented. Second, understanding is worked out in joint action with others, through shared but not necessarily articulated understandings of "what is real, what is privilege, what is problem, and what is moral" (p. 24).[3] Thus the process of knowing is essentially embodied, realized through action, and therefore often worked out in a domain beyond consciousness. This fundamentally challenges the belief that individual reflection and memory are significant in knowledge production.

Truth claims become problematic in situative views. Here, knowledge is not judged by what is "true" and "false," or what is "erroneous," but by what is relevant in this particular situation, what is worth knowing and doing, what is convenient for whom, and what to do next (Lave & Chaiklin, 1993). The emphasis is on improving one's ability to *participate meaningfully* in particular practices, and moving to legitimate roles within communities. What is meaningful must be negotiated between the individual's desires and intentions (including the desire to belong), and the community's changing requirements for certain forms of participation. Situated theorists focus their continuing inquiry on questions such as, What constitutes meaningful action for a particular individual in a given context? How is the development of knowledge constrained or created by the intersection of several existing practices in a particular space? (Lave & Wenger, 1991). The outcome of experiential learning as participation is that the *community* refines its practices, develops new ones, or discards and changes practices that are harmful or dysfunctional. For individuals within communities, argue some situative theorists, the experiential learning process of becoming a full participant helps develop the ability to participate more easily in other situations.

Critics of the situative view, however, have raised concerns about the monitoring of a community's practices: What about patterns and procedures that are harmful, unjust, exclusive, or just plain dysfunctional in preventing the community from fulfilling its core purposes? What about inequitable opportunities to participate in a community—how do those who are excluded or marginalized become more fully involved? And what about traditions—how does a community break free from habitual practices that become rigidly resistant to improvement or change? Others have wondered how the situative view accounts for the ways power flows through a community, granting control to some, garnering conflict among others, and maintaining hegemonic beliefs and norms of acting. Coming back to the individual in a community of practice, critics claim that clearly there are complex layers to consider in terms of a person's subjectivity—including inner longings, fears, and conflicts that influence our motive and ability to participate in practices. These are addressed by psychoanalytic theories of experiential learning.

ATTUNING TO UNCONSCIOUS DESIRES AND FEARS
(Psychoanalytic Theory of Learning)

Psychoanalytic theory has been taken up by educational theorists in the late twentieth century to help disrupt notions of progressive development, certainty of knowledge, and the centered individual learner. Psychoanalytic theory also helps open ways of approaching the realm of the unconscious; our resis-

tances to knowledge; the desire for closure and mastery that
sometimes governs the educational impulse; and enigmatic tensions between learner, knowledge, and educator. A prominent
theme is the individual's relationship between the outside world
of culture and objects of knowledge, and the inside world of
psychic energies and dilemmas of relating to these objects of
knowledge. Object relations theory, as Melanie Klein has explained, shows how the ego negotiates its boundaries with these
objects.[4]

According to psychoanalytic learning theorists, the inside
world is configured by dilemmas. These unfold through struggles between the unconscious, and the conscious mind which is
aware of unconscious rumblings but can neither access them
fully nor understand their language. Deborah Britzman (1998b)
describes the unconscious as an "impossible concept" that cannot be educated: "knows no time, knows no negation, knows
no contradiction . . . We do not address the unconscious, it ad-
dresses us. But its grammar is strange and dreamy; it resists its
own unveiling" (p. 55). The conscious mind, on the other hand,
is both ignorant and partially aware of its own ignorance. The
consciousness is thus anxious about its own uncertain, impar-
tial knowledge, its limited ability to know, and its fragile boundaries and existence. This anxiety often generates resistance to
learning, as for example when we fight concepts which, even if
we suspect their value, fundamentally challenge our existing beliefs or draw us into questions we would rather not pursue. The
resulting negation or repression of certain knowledges holds
particular interest for psychoanalytic learning theorists.[5]

Britzman's (1998a) theory views experiential learning as
interference of conscious thought by the unconscious, and the
uncanny psychic conflicts that result. Our deep desires for and
resistances to different objects, which we experience as matters
of love and hate, attach our internal world to the external social
world. We long to know some things, to possess some things,
or to be desired by some things, driving us to act in particular
ways that we may not be aware of to pursue these longings. For
example, as teachers we may want learners to like us, or wish
they would desire to know what we know. While we may deny

having such longings or being affected by their frustration, such desires may drive us to behaviors that are inconsistent with our rational beliefs about good teaching. Our daily, disturbing inside-outside encounters are carried on at subtle levels and we draw upon many strategies to ignore them.[6] Thus, as Lisa Loutzenheiser (2001) writes in her examination of antiracist teaching, ignorance is not a passive lack of knowledge but involves a type of Othering, pushing away that which we do not want to know. But when we truly attend these encounters we enter the profound conflicts that are learning.

Although the unconscious can't be known directly, its workings interfere with our intentions and our conscious perception of direct experience. These workings constantly bother the ego, producing breaches between acts, thoughts, wishes, and responsibility. Despite the ego's varied and creative defenses against confronting these breaches, the conscious mind is forced to notice random paradoxes and contradictions of experience, and uncanny slips into sudden awareness of difficult truths about the self. These truths are what Britzman (1998a) calls "lost subjects," those parts of our selves that we resist, then try to reclaim and want to explore, but are afraid to. True knowledge of these lost and perhaps disturbing parts of ourselves jeopardizes our ego's conscious sense of itself as a self-determined, sensible, knowledgeable self. But, for the self to be more than a prisoner of its own narcissism, it must bother itself, notice the breaches between acts, thoughts, dreams, waking, wishes, and responsibility. We learn by *working through* the conflicts of all these psychic events that comprise "difficult knowledge." Adult learning is thus coming to tolerate one's own conflicting desires, while recovering the selves that are repressed from our terror of full self-knowledge.

Critics wonder what happens to societal change when too much emphasis is placed on the individual's psychic dramas (Saltman, 1998). Some question the existence of an unconscious realm, and ask for clearer definition of it. Instead of the unconscious, Elana Michelson (1999) prefers to talk about sites of transgression, where experience exceeds the boundaries of sociocultural norms and language: "the surfeit of experience after all authorized meanings have been exhausted, the excess that enables and contests every performance and affirms the unruly intractable element in experience" (p. 149). The contribution of psychoanalytic theory to experiential learning is its demonstration of the limits of conscious reflection on lived experience. The focus on the reflecting rational mind by constructivists may overlook what Elizabeth Ellsworth (1997) describes as "chasms opened up by lived experience that map onto no known or authorized concepts, words, or arguments" (p. 188). Psychoanalytic learning theory attempts to map certain complex dimensions of this experience in which personal transformation can occur. Those seeking societal transformation tend to promote critical cultural theories of experiential learning.

RESISTING DOMINANT SOCIAL NORMS
OF EXPERIENCE
(Critical Cultural Theories)

Critical cultural perspectives center *power* as a core issue in experience, and *transformation* (of oppressive beliefs and social structures) through learning. The problem with some situated views and systems-theory perspectives is their lack of attention to inevitable power relations and the resulting inequities and repressions circulating in human cultural systems. Any system is a complex site of competing cultures. To understand human learning we must, from a critical cultural perspective, analyse the ideologies and other structures of dominance that express or govern the social relationships, and competing forms of communication and cultural practices within that system. Writers in critical cultural pedagogy (such as Allman, 2001; Freire, 1970; Giroux, 1992; Giroux & McLaren, 1994; Gore, 1993; hooks, 1994; Kellner, 1995; Lather, 1991; McLaren, 1989; Welton, 1995) claim that when these mechanisms of cultural power are named, ways and means to resist them appear. With resistance people can become open to unexpected, unimagined possibilities for work, life, and development.

Michael Welton (1995), a Canadian adult educator and

historian, presents a theory of critical social learning based on the theories of Jurgen Habermas. Welton focuses on how adults "unlearn their socialization to support and reproduce an unjust and unfree society, and learn to be enlightened, empowered and transformative actors in particular times and places" (p. 26–27). Human potential is too often blocked or distorted by existing institutions and forms of communicative action (in work, consumption, education, families, and commodified civil spaces) that are non-democratic and non-developmental. That is, when adults participate in systems and exchanges where power is unequally distributed, where the focus is on technical rational control and where they are unaware of their own human potential, they shrivel. Critical learning is a process of throwing off the beliefs that imprison our lifeworlds of meanings and culture, and reclaiming our autonomy and capability as self-determining citizens. This learning may be triggered by a felt crisis in our private or public experience that threatens a sense of social integration, and motivates us to release this potential. The process of learning occurs not only through critical reflection but also in democratic dialogue, practical moral insights, or relationships and activities that we work to make more generative and reciprocal. Collective action for social justice such as movements for peace, environmental sustainability, race and gender equity, or workers claiming control over the means of production, may be prompted by critical learning but may or may not foster developmental learning. Following Habermas, Welton asks of any cultural site, whether dedicated to political action or not, To what extent is this enabling critically reflective or "developmental" learning that truly emancipates people? Stephen Brookfield (2001, 2002a, 2002b) also provides a clear overview of some core concepts of critical theory in terms of adult learning explaining its Marxist roots and describing contributions of critical theorists.

As Michel Foucault (1980) has shown, it is simplistic to conceive power as domination or an irrevocable force determining human activity. Critical cultural studies offer tools for tracing complex power relations and their consequences. The field is wide and certainly not monolithic, embracing feminism, ideology critique, critical discourse analysis, critical media studies, post-colonialism and subaltern studies, antiracism theory, technoculture theory, and others. Obviously many conflicting perspectives and emphases are involved. For the purpose of this brief section, little distinction will be made among these perspectives although their heterogeneity should remain understood. Their writers all have in common their belief that politics are central to human cognition, activity, identity, and meaning. They expose existing moment-to-moment interplays of power, and advocate social reconstruction by seeking more inclusive, generative, and integrative alternatives to oppressive cultural practices and discourses.

Some critical cultural perspectives suggest that learning in a particular cultural space is shaped by the *discourses and their semiotics* (the signs, codes, and texts) that are most visible and accorded most authority by different groups. These discourses often create dualistic categories such as man/woman, reflection/action, learning/doing, formal/informal that determine unequal distribution of authority and resources. Such dualisms can result in labels that depersonalize human beings. They also endow certain institutions with legitimacy and exclude others, by representing "norms" and casting nonconformists as "other" to these norms. Analysts such as Douglas Kellner (1995) show how such *representations* of people in cultural discourses contain, define, control behavior and relations, and generally limit the possibilities of people's identities. Robert Young (1990) suggests that learning should include understanding the historical forces and mythologies that have shaped these discourses and representations, including the experiences and contributions of both winners and losers, as these are defined by a discourse.

Critical writers ask, What social and cultural capital is valued most in a particular community, and which group is reflected in it? If we find ourselves "learning" to become competent in achieving values of continuous consumption, wealth accumulation, middle class norms of dress, speech, family, home, privacy, and entertainment, we help to reproduce a system that endows these ideals with cultural capital. Our learning pursuits are shaped and enabled by social networks, trust and contacts—

the social capital accrued through belonging to a particular group. Those excluded from circles that provide learning opportunities to develop this capital are ignored, pronounced deviant, or targeted for fixing by well-meaning educational programs. Knowledge itself and the categories that make it possible are capital invested with values. Critics ask, What is considered legitimate knowledge among a particular group or a whole society? Which kinds and whose knowledge count most—in higher education, in different workplaces, in community and family life? We might then look more closely at how certain forms of habituated, ongoing experiential learning—without critical assessment and redirection—merely perpetuates existing systems of knowledge that are valued and easily accessed only by certain groups. Those who have experientially learned other forms of knowledge have little way of participating socially with members of these powerful groups.

For Marxist critical educators such as Paula Allman (2001), people should transform these social relations through learning in collective action. In her book *Critical Education Against Global Capitalism*, Allman describes the principles of such learning to include mutual respect (developed as people support one another in transformation), commitment to reading the world critically and acting to change it, honesty, vigilance, and passion for justice. The purposes of this critical experiential learning are, above all, to develop critical, creative, and hopeful thinking towards a transformation of self and existing social relations. Allman herself writes passionately about this learning as a collaborative, participatory process, where people experientially learn to depend on one another to see the larger problems in their everyday lives. They then are encouraged to work together to fight dehumanizing conditions and create a more democratic, equitable, sustainable reality. The starting point is challenging those naturalized definitions and categories through which we learn experientially to separate and polarize ourselves from others, or to assure our success and comfort at the expense of others.

Thus, *borders and boundaries* are significant for critical cultural writers in different ways than for theorists of other perspectives in which boundaries between inner and outer worlds (psychoanalytic), or between individual knower and objects of the environment (constructivist) are of most interest. Henry Giroux (1992), for example, analyses borders that are perceived to define cultural communities and territories, examining the identity options constructed for people within certain borders and the consequences for those who transgress. New spaces for alternative cultural practices and identities are being opened by border crossings in this globalized world, and boundaries between real and virtual cultures, individual and collective experiences, are increasingly blurred. These issues raise questions about the places of experience and spaces of learning, which may be far more fluid or hybrid than some critical theories portray. Perhaps society is not so easily divided into groups that are dominant or oppressed, perhaps people are more than the product of particular ideologies, discourses and cultural practices, and perhaps identities and knowledge change as circumstances shift. Some theorists seeking robust explanations for this fluidity are turning to complexity theory to explore ecological understandings of how knowledge develops in systems.

EXPLORING ECOLOGICAL RELATIONSHIPS BETWEEN COGNITION AND ENVIRONMENT (Complexity Theories Applied to Learning)

Ecological perspectives explain learning as the *co-emergence* of learner and setting (Maturana & Varela, 1987; Varela, Thompson, & Rosch, 1991). Based on complexity theory and enaction theory, this view assumes that cognition depends on the kinds of experience that come from having a body with various sensori-motor capacities embedded in a biological, psychological, cultural context. Ecological theorists explore how cognition and environment become *simultaneously enacted* through experiential learning. The first premise is that the systems represented by person and context are inseparable, and the second is that change occurs from emerging systems affected by the intentional tinkering of one with the other, particularly in the disturbances created by their interactions.

This understanding of co-emergent cognition, identities, and environment begins by stepping aside from constructivist notions of knowledge as a substantive thing to be acquired or developed by learners as isolated cognitive agents, thereafter to exist *within* them. Brent Davis and Dennis Sumara (1997) explain that instead, complexity theorists believe that "cognition exists in the *interstices* of a complex ecology or organismic relationality" (p. 110). Humans are understood to form part of the context itself, as systems that are completely interconnected with the systems in which they act. Humberto Maturana and Francesco Varela (1987) have represented the unfolding of this interconnection as a series of structural couplings. When two systems coincide, the perturbations of one system excites responses in the structural dynamics of the other. The resultant coupling creates a new transcendent unity of action and identities that could not have been achieved independently by either participant.

Educators might understand this phenomenon through the example of conversation, a collective activity in which interaction enfolds the participants and moves beyond them in a "commingling of consciousness" (Davis & Sumara, 1997). As each contributes, changing the conversational dynamic, other participants are changed, the relational space among them all changes, and the looping-back changes the contributor. This is "mutual specification" (Varela, Thompson, & Rosch, 1991), the fundamental dynamic of systems constantly engaging in joint action and interaction. As actors are influenced by symbols and actions in which they participate, they adapt and learn. As they do so, their behaviors and thus their effects upon the systems connected with them change. With each change these complex systems shift, changing their patterns of interaction and the individual identities of all actors enmeshed in them. Thus the environment and the learner emerge together in the process of cognition, although this is a false dichotomy: there is no *context* separate from any particular system such as an individual actor. Brent

Davis, Dennis Sumara and Rebecca Luce-Kapler (2000) describe co-emergence as "a new understanding of cognition":

> Rather than being cast as a locatable process or phenomenon, cognition has been reinterpreted as a joint participation, a choreography. An agent's knowing, in this sense, are [sic] those patterns of acting that afford it a coherence—that is, that make it discernible as a unity, a wholeness, identity. The question, "Where does cognition happen?" is thus equivalent to, "Who or what is perceived to be acting?" In this way, a rain forest is cognitive—and humanity is necessarily participating in its cogitations/evolutions. That is, our habits of thought are entwined and implicated in unfolding global conditions. (p. 74)

The apparent similarity of this with situated perspectives articulated by Lave and Wenger (1991) or James Greeno (1997) rests in this primacy granted to environment as integrated with cognition, not simply supplemental to the individual consciousness. However, there are fundamental distinctions. Where situated cognition arose within the discipline of psychology, enactivism is rooted in evolutionary biology. Situated cognition is therefore anthropocentric, premised upon and scrutinizing an individual subject who *develops* through a movement of participation in a community of practice. The interactions comprising participation form the integration of person and context, but autonomous subjectivity and the concept of individual mind remain privileged and fundamentally unchallenged. The person *learns to* participate more effectively by participating. Complexity theory on the other hand is premised on systems theory, understanding planetary evolution through multiple systems enmeshed in processes of self-organization and interdependence. Change (such as phenomena that other perspectives may observe as learning) occurs through disturbances amplified through feedback loops within and among systems.

Ecological perspectives consider understandings to be embedded in conduct. Davis and Sumara (1997) explain this premise by drawing attention to the knowledge we are constantly enacting as we move through the world. Often called habit or tacit knowledge by others, enactivists view these understandings as existing not within ourselves in ways that drive our actions, but as unfolding in circumstances that evoke these particular actions. As example, Davis and Sumara show how a "choreography of movement" can be discerned in a particular community, where individuals find themselves swept up in collective patterns of expectation and behavior. Their examples show how much of this joint action exceeds and leaks out of individual attempts to attend to and control unconscious action through critical reflection. The problem lies not in underdeveloped critical abilities that should be educated, but in a false conceptualization of the learning *figure* as separate from the contextual *ground*. Ecological perspectives draw attention to the background, and examine myriad fluctuations, subtle interactions, imaginings and intuitions, the invisible implied by the visible, and the series of consequences emerging from any single action. All of these we normally relegate to the backdrop of our focus on whatever we construe to be the significant learning event. But the focus of ecological perspectives is not on the components of experience (which other perspectives might describe in fragmented terms: person, experience, tools, community, and activity) but on the *relationships* binding them together in complex systems.

Learning is thus cast as continuous invention and exploration, produced through the relations among consciousness, identity, action and interaction, objects, and structural dynamics of complex systems. There is no absolute standard of conduct, because conduct flows ceaselessly. Maturana and Varela (1987) suggest that subsystems in a series of increasingly complex systems together invent changing understandings of what is "adequate conduct" in this particular time and situation, or "consensual domain" (p. 39). "Adequate conduct" is action that serves a particular consensual domain. New possibilities for action are constantly emerging among the interactions of complex systems, and thus cognition occurs in the possibility for unpredictable shared action. Knowledge cannot be contained in any one element or dimension of a system, for knowledge is constantly emerging and spilling into other systems. Learning is then defined as "a process through which one becomes capable of more sophisticated, more flexible, more creative action" (Davis, Sumara, & Luce-Kapler, 2000, p. 73).

CONCLUSION

This chapter has provided a brief overview of five alternative perspectives that raise important questions about the nature of experience. The constructivist theory of experiential learning emphasizes individual construction of knowledge through personal reflection in or on action. The situative perspective understands experiential learning as increasingly full participation in a community of practice. Psychoanalytic theories draw our attention to inner dimensions beyond the reach of our rational consciousness, and encourage learning through confronting and coming to understand unconscious desires and fears. Critical cultural perspectives advocate for experiential learning that seeks to transform existing social orders, by critically questioning and resisting dominant norms of experience. Finally, ecological approaches offer a view of experiential human learning as intimately connected not only with other humans but also with the changing objects and forms of the systems in which they interact. Those perspectives encourage greater focus on clarifying and nurturing the ecological relationships between cognition and environment. For those interested in further discussion, Chapters 3 and 4 provide more in-depth exploration of particular questions and debates within and among these theoretical perspectives.

Table 2.1 summarizes the differences among these five perspectives. The table's dimensions have been discussed in the descriptions of each of the five perspectives: the primary focus in learning, the basic explanatory schemata each uses to explain learning, how each views the nature of knowledge and the production of experience, how each understands the relationships of learners to objects and situations of knowing, how each believes the learning process actually occurs, each view about what constitutes important learning goals and outcomes, and each view of power and politics in experience and knowing.[7]

There are many problems and ironies in presenting complex theoretical perspectives in chart form. Ideas that blur together appear to be naturally separate and even opposite. Complex nuances are reduced to simple terms. Conflicting ideas are rolled together under a single heading. The focus on a limited number of dimensions eliminates other dimensions which some may consider significant. There is also an inherent difficulty in applying any single dimension to interpret multiple perspectives, for each perspective is its own world with its own defining schemata. Within its own world, any single perspective here would subsume, interpret, and classify the others in particular ways.[8] Finally, even the act of comparing one with another is potentially problematic. The equalized side-by-side representation of these categories masks the differential influence each wields on adult education practice, on social theory, and on each other.

These are the compromises of presenting different theoretical perspectives comparatively, and presenting a chart to aid understanding and help produce a certain clarity. This comparison may help interrupt and extend our thinking about teaching and learning. This is a temporary classification, a starting point intending to illuminate openings where serious questions may be raised and dialogue encouraged among perspectives regarding experiential learning.

NOTES

1. Phillips (1995) identifies six distinct views of constructivism ranging according to the emphasis accorded either to individual psychology or public disciplines in constructing knowledge; the extent to which knowledge is viewed as made rather than discovered; and the emphasis put on the individual knower as active agent rather than spectator in the construction of knowledge.
2. In particular *activity theory,* which builds on Vygotskian ideas, has been widely used to understand learning in educational as well as workplace contexts. Yrjö Engeström, a major proponent of activity theory, shows how learning involves a subject in some kind of goal-oriented action mediated by some kind of object or tool. The subject, whether one person or a group, is socially constructed, the

Table 2.1 Overview of Five Theoretical Orientations of Experiential Learning: Distinguishing Characteristics

Perspective	Focus and Key Questions	Explanatory Schemata	View of Knowledge
Reflecting upon concrete experience **Constructivist theory**	• Focus is on how individuals construct meanings from their experiences to produce knowledge.	• Processes and structures of perception, memory, belief structures, and interpretation. • Reflective analysis of personal assumptions. • Processes of belief transformation.	• Individual mind: A set of mental constructs that can be represented, expressed, and transferred to new situations.
Participating in a community of practice **Situative theory**	• Focus is on practices in which individuals have learned to participate. • What constitutes meaningful action for a particular individual in a given context? • How do people learn adaptively in situations where they engage in activities?	• Interactive systems, including individuals as participants. • Properties of social practices: collaborative work, distribution of accountability and authority, information sources, characteristics of interaction.	• Participation with increasing effectiveness. • Knowledge is not judged by what is "true" or "erroneous" but by what is relevant here, what is worth knowing and doing, what is convenient for whom, and what to do next in this particular situation.
Attuning to unconscious desires and fears **Psychoanalytic theory**	• Focus is on the self—how it is crafted, repressed, recovered, understood. • How does the unconscious interfere with conscious thought to produce knowledge?	• Unconscious desires and insights. • Ego's self-protective defenses. • Vicissitudes of love and hate in learning. • Internal conflicts.	• Passionate tensions of love and hate. • New versions of old conflicts. • Dynamic psychical events.
Resisting dominant social norms of experience **Critical cultural theories**	• Focus is on how power circulates to repress or enhance experience and learning. • How is identity limited or liberated by prevailing cultural codes?	• Cultural practices, cultural capital, and discourses. • Regulation and distribution of authority and resources. • Experience is shaped by the circulation of power, dominant groups' interests, and other groups' resistance.	• Knowledge is emancipation from passive acceptance of received identities and dominant cultural structures. • Knowledge is expressed through resistance (in voice, action, or silence).
Exploring ecological relationships between cognition and environment **Complexity theories**	• Focus is on co-emergence of systems (learner, setting). • How do cognition and environment become simultaneously enacted?	• Learner is a complex adaptive system, comprised of subsystems, and nested in larger systems. • Complex systems are self-organizing, emergent, expansive. • Healthy systems rely upon diverse parts continually creating and adapting.	• Cognition is embodied enaction: a history of structural coupling that brings forth a world. • Knowledge is contingent and contextual, always evolving. • Learners' identities are inseparable from their activities and knowledge.

Table 2.1 *(continued)*

Relation of Learner to Object/Context of Knowing	Learning Process	Learning Purposes and Desired Outcomes	Nature of Power in Experience and Knowing
• Learner inquires and experiments, guided by personal intention. • Situation presents possibilities from which learner selects objects of knowing.	• Constructing personal understanding from action in the world. • Through reflection on experience, learner creates relevant structures of meaning.	• Develop more inclusive, integrative, discriminating mental constructs which can enable individual's success in new situations.	• Power may repress individual's own personal constructions, and alienate learner from value of own experiences.
• Social and individual skills and activity are inseparable. • Knowing does not exist apart from the tools, community, and activity of a particular situation.	• Becoming more attuned to constraints and affordances of particular situations. • Learner progresses along trajectories of participation and growth of identity.	• Improve participation in interactive systems, in social practices valued most by the learner/community. • Participation becomes more meaningful personally, socially.	• Learner moves from peripheral participation in a community to more central positionality, with competence. • Pedagogy that separates learning from doing is artificial, repressive.
• Internal conflicts are new versions of old cultural conflicts. • Internal world (psychic) is attached to outside (social) through matters of love and hate. • Inside-outside encounters produce the conflicts which are learning.	• Unlearning old strategies of survival. • Working through dilemmas to explore one's desires, attachments, self, and resistances to knowing.	• Come to tolerate the demands of the self and the social. • Come to accept and understand (recovered) selves. • Become aware of deep desires and fears, and find more productive ways to satisfy them.	• Interference must occur within the learner. • Pedagogy is viewed as repressive, and intolerant of complex processes of psychic working-through. • Conflicts at the point where learners meet the force of their cultural history stimulate interference.
• Learner's positionality is political. • Power relations determine learner's relation to situation and object of knowing. • Learners' sense of experience is shaped by powerful cultural discourses and practices.	• Naming repressive cultural practices and discourses. • Linking personal experience of oppression to larger forces. • Acting with others to create a more democratic, equitable, sustainable society. • Recovering lost subject positions and voice.	• Work towards social reconstruction. • Understand the politics, constraints, and effects of cultural practices on personal experience and identity. • Support insurgent resistance to oppression. • Build coalitions among differences towards collective solidarity.	• The way power flows in a particular relationship and culture determines knowledge. • Power determines what is considered knowable and worth knowing, who is a recognizable knower, the conditions and meanings of experience.
• Learner's perceptions are experiential and enacted within complex systems. • Subsystems of the learner are embedded in networks of the context. • Focus is on relationships *between* elements of the system—learner, objects, other actors, environment systems, etc.	• All parts of the system are continuously learning. • As one part copes with new situations and conditions, it changes behavior which influences changes in the parts around it. • Disturbance in any system part, when amplified, affects learning of all parts.	• Describe and analyse learning in systems. • Become more capable of more sophisticated, more flexible, more creative action.	• Power is understood in terms of system dynamics, as energy. • Power is continuous, generative, creative.

action is situated in a collective system which is also socially constructed and governed by particular rules, and the tools are culturally and historically produced. All three dimensions of this system
are transformed through the activity which is ongoing. There is no
static "learner" or clear separation of internal and external processes.

3. Pile and Thrift are part of a current in cultural geography that is
    using metaphors of space, movement, maps, and time to analyse
    subjectivity and learning. *Actor-network theory* is one frame that
    has generated recent pedagogical interest. As described by writers
    like Bruno Latour (1993), actor-network theory illuminates re-
    gional flows of action in terms of knowledge production. Knowl-
    edge is viewed as constituted in networks of people and objects
    spread across space and time; individuals develop as they move
    through these networks. Individuals experience the network's knowl-
    edge as they participate in its spatial and temporal arrangements.
    The space-time arrangements of a particular activity have physical
    and symbolic dimensions, representing to individuals what they are
    supposed to do in a space and how they should use their time (in-
    cluding notions of who or what is not supposed to be there).

4. According to object relations theory, once the ego perceives an ob-
    ject as distinct from itself, it decides whether to desire the object as
    "good" or reject it as "bad": "perception is thus an ego function
    that responds both to the demands of unconscious desire and to the
    external demands of reality" (Gilbert, 1998, p. 31). The next deci-
    sion is whether to ingest the "good" object or not. Knowledge per-
    ceived as "good" is still threatening, for once it is taken *in* to the
    ego it has the potential to transform the ego—an event against
    which the ego tries to protect itself. The ego also risks destroying
    the good object of knowledge through the act of incorporating it,
    and losing the boundaries that separate itself from the knowledge.

5. Freud argued that intolerable ideas are permitted into the con-
    sciousness only as our denial that the idea is true. In this denial we
    attempt to intellectualize the idea, to separate our ego's emotional
    involvement with (and therefore possible subjection to) the idea,
    even while we are actively "hating" the idea. In these tensions be-
    tween intellection and affection, learning occurs as a movement
    through the dilemma to accepting the knowledge. The dynamic of
    pedagogy within this movement is problematic. Should education
    induce these tensions and somehow midwife the movement to
    learner's acknowledgment and insight? How much anxiety can an

individual stand? How can learning proceed if its very conditions of anxiety stimulate the resistance that forestalls learning?

6. Britzman calls these survival strategies the "arts of getting by," and claims they are prevalent in education. Curriculum mostly resists these complex subtle encounters constantly playing beneath classroom talk in the press of "covering" content, and both students and teachers have learned to ignore them.

7. These dimensions were suggested by other classifications of cognitive perspectives: Greeno's (1997) response to debates about the nature of situated knowing; Davis and Sumara's (1997) comparison of cognitivism, constructivism and enactivism; and Mezirow's (1996) discussion of three "contemporary paradigms of learning."

8. For examples of this very phenomena, see Mezirow (1996) who subsumes other theories of cognition under a preferred perspective "transformative learning"; and debates on cognition published in the *Educational Researcher* (Anderson, Reder & Simon, 1996; Greeno, 1997; Prawat, 1993) in which different writers assess each other's perspectives according to the postulates of their own premises.

CHAPTER 3

How and What Do People Learn from Experience?

So, *how* do people learn through their experiences? All of the five different perspectives introduced in Chapter 2 have a slightly different response, and their explanations each contribute interesting considerations about the psyche, politics, systems, and situations of learning. But we are still left with fundamental questions cutting across perspectives. How are reflection and transformation involved in experiential learning? And what are the connections between learning and doing, learner and context? How is experiential learning interrelated with communities, social relationships, culture, and diversity? Where are the body and desire in experiential learning? How is learning part of complex systems? And what can be said about transfer of learning, if such a process exists?

This chapter continues to build on the five perspectives of constructivist, situative, psychoanalytic, critical cultural, and ecological approaches to experiential learning by addressing these types of questions. In some cases theorists have developed models to answer a question, and certain well-known models of experiential learning are outlined here. While useful for educators, these models have become the focus for critical debates expanded in the next chapter. So at this point, we should read not only to uncover possibilities for practice, but also critically, to locate inconsistencies, oversights, simplistic answers, and contradictions.

HOW IS REFLECTION INVOLVED IN LEARNING THROUGH EXPERIENCE?

As we saw in Chapter 2, the constructivist view understands learning to occur through reflection upon a lived experience. In adult learning literature, this view is embedded in the writings of David Boud and associates (1996), David Kolb (1984), Dorothy MacKeracher (1996), Jack Mezirow (1990), Donald Schön (1983), and many others. Kolb (1984) developed a theory to clarify exactly how different people learn by integrating their concrete emotional experiences with reflection. For him, reflection is all about cognitive processes of conceptual analysis and eventual understanding. Kolb believed that experiential learning is a tension and conflict-filled process, and occurs in a cycle. New knowledge and skills are achieved through confrontation among concrete experience, reflective observation, abstract conceptualization, and subsequent active experimentation.

First, the learner lives through some kind of **concrete experience**. This could be a simulated experience developed especially for a learning situation, such as a case study or role-play, or an exercise involving the learner in actually experimenting with the skills to be learned. Or this could be a real-life or workplace experience that the learner has encountered. Second, the learner takes some time for **reflective observation**. The learner asks of the experience: What did I observe? What was I aware of? What does this experience mean to me? How might this experience have been different? Third, the learner uses insights gained through the reflective observation to create an **abstract conceptualization**. This is where the learner asks, What principle seems to be operating here? What general rule-of-thumb have I learned here? What new understanding does this experience reveal about myself, or people, or how things work in particular situations? Finally, the learner applies the new learning through **active experimentation**. The learner asks, What will I do next time? How will I adopt this principle for other contexts? The new principle is tested out in similar situations, then in different situations, and the learner continues to revise and reshape the learning based on what happens through experimenting with it. The learner may not actually test out the new skill, but may simply think through its application.

Kolb and other theorists contend that although all adults are exposed to a multitude of life experiences, not everyone learns from these. Learning happens only when there is reflective thought and internal processing of that experience by the learner, in a way that actively makes sense of the experience, that links the experience to previous learning, and that transforms the learner's previous understandings in some way.

Donald Schön (1983, 1987) has been a significant promoter of constructivism to understand workplace learning. Schön's view is that professionals live in a world of uncertainty, instability, complexity, and value conflict, where they often must deal with problems for which no existing rules or theories learned through formal training or past experience can apply. He was most interested in how reflection, and particularly critical reflection, plays out in the ongoing learning of professionals in their practice. He argued that practitioners learn by noticing and framing problems of interest to them in particular ways, then inquiring and experimenting with solutions. When they experience surprise or discomfort in their everyday activity, this reflective process begins. Their knowledge is constructed through reflection during and after some experimental action on the ill-defined and messy problems of practice.

When these adults meet such unique problems or situations containing some element of surprise, they are prompted to *reflect in action* by improvising an on-the-spot experimentation, thinking up and testing out and refining and retesting various solutions for the problem. Schön says professionals also often *reflect on action* in some zone of time after a problem-episode, when they examine what they did, how they did it, and what alternatives exist. Other theorists of learning have continued to refine Schön's ideas of reflective practice. David Boud and David Walker (1991) emphasized the importance of an individual's readiness to learn from an experience, and that individual's attention to feelings in reflection. Victoria Marsick and Karen Watkins (1992) formulated a theoretical framework of informal and incidental learning to show how a person's experiential learning is not always conscious, and may simply reproduce the (sometimes dysfunctional or erroneous) beliefs of the surrounding contexts. Marsick and Watkins stress the importance of Schön's notion of critical reflection to test the assumptions of our reflections and lead us to important changes in how we think and act.

WHEN DOES EXPERIENTIAL LEARNING TRANSFORM OUR THINKING AND ACTING?

In the everyday process of meaning-making and problem-solving, constructivist theory explains that we learn procedural knowledge (how to do things or solve problems) and propositional knowledge (what things mean) through reflecting on experiences. But critical reflection, says Schön, is more than simply reflecting in or reflecting on action. When people engage in critical reflection they question how they framed the problem in the first place. Even if no apparent problems exist, the practitioner questions situations, asking why things are the way they are, why events unfold in the way they do. This is critical reflection to probe what otherwise are taken-for-granted situations. As well, people reflect critically when they evaluate their own actions, asking: Why did I do what I did? What beliefs inform my practice, and how are these beliefs helping or hindering my work? Schön's work celebrated the experiential learning of practitioners in everyday action—what he called the swampy lowlands of actual practice—and attempted to challenge the high road of theoretical knowledge and "technical rationality" over which universities hold authority.

Stephen Brookfield (1987, 1995) and Jack Mezirow (1991) both have made considerable contributions to constructivist views of adult learning by theorizing how critical reflection interrupts, reconstructs, and thus transforms human beliefs. Brookfield (1987) suggested that when we reflect on our experience with skeptical questioning and imaginative speculation, we could refine, deepen, or correct our knowledge constructions. He described three stages in the process of reflecting critically: "(1)

identifying the assumptions that underlie our thoughts and actions; (2) scrutinizing the accuracy and validity of these in terms of how they connect to, or are discrepant with, our experience of reality; and (3) reconstituting these assumptions to make them more inclusive and integrative" (p. 177). The key is confronting and perhaps rupturing one's deepest beliefs. This raises a question: Why would individuals intent upon protecting and strengthening their beliefs willingly subject them to painful confrontation? Sharan Merriam and Barbara Heuer (1996) suggest that humans are driven by a compelling impulse to search for meaning, and particularly the meaning of life, a quest fueled by people's deep need to make sense and coherence out of life. The meanings that result are rooted in each person's context, from a dynamic interplay between an individual's identity and personal experience. This meaning-making process leads to development of self when some aspect of experience and self is challenged.

In 1978 Jack Mezirow presented a theory of learning, explained exhaustively in his book *Transformative Dimensions of Adult Learning* (1991), where reflection on experience and particularly critical reflection are central. Transformative learning has become one of the most influential ideas in the field of adult learning and development to emerge in the past 20 years. Mezirow has continued to argue, throughout the exhaustive debates gathering around his theory,[1] that when individuals experience a major disorienting experience causing them to reflectively reconsider the fundamental understandings comprising their worldviews (formed through their biographies of experience), they transform these basic knowledge structures or meaning perspectives to become more "inclusive, differentiating, permeable, critically reflective, and integrative of experience" (Mezirow, 1991, p. 14). This process of perspective transformation is fundamentally based upon a "reflective assessment of premises . . . [and] of movement through cognitive structures by identifying and judging presuppositions . . . Reflection is the apperceptive process by which we change our minds, literally and figuratively" (Mezirow as cited by Taylor, 1998, pp. 5, 9).

Mezirow's theory of transformative learning is based on a

tri-level concept of critical reflection on experience. Mezirow suggests that when an adult encounters a disorienting dilemma, a problem for which there is no immediately apparent solution suggested by past experience and knowledge, reflection is often triggered. First, individuals often reflect on the *content* of the experience—what happened?—that may or may not lead to learning. If individuals find and test a solution to the problem that produces undesirable outcomes, they often reflect upon the *process* they employed—how did it happen?. Thus procedural learning results as learners analyse and learn from faulty choices. But when the reflection probes the very *premises* (deep-seated beliefs and assumptions guiding action) upon which we have based our problemsolving, then critical reflection results. Others' views can act as mirrors for our own views, opening a dialectic, helping us "unfreeze" our "meaning perspectives" (Mezirow, 1991) and assumptions. In this third level of reflection we confront and challenge the taken-for-granted norms—what's wrong with how I am seeing what happened and how it happened?—leading to a dramatic shift or *transformation* in the learner's way of viewing the world. Mezirow (1991) describes this process of transformative learning as the "bringing of one's assumptions, premises, criteria, and schemata into consciousness and vigorously critiquing them" (p. 29). For example, Gordon Ball (1999) describes the transformative learning of people who had developed a global ecological perspective of life. Most had become immersed in new, unsettling, and unfamiliar circumstances such as a foreign culture, a disadvantaged group or a gross injustice, followed by deep and intense emotion. Over time, writes Ball, all experienced transformation to a new passionate commitment, through ethics, action, and identity, to a sustainable interconnected philosophy of life.

This transformative learning is described by Brookfield (2001), in his more recent writings developing a critical theory of adult learning, as centrally motivated by "the desire to extend democratic socialist values and processes, to create a world in which a commitment to the common good is the foundations of individual well-being and adult development" (p. 21). This desire is fundamental in popular education or forms of transformative political learning that Shahrzad Mojab (2001) calls revolutionary critical education. Both are based on helping adults to transform their interpretation of problems they have personally experienced and learn, through social action, how to build new social formations. Groups are facilitated to share their problematic experiences in dialogue, and analyze how issues such as unemployment, divorce, discrimination, work intensification, or unhappiness are not necessarily personal failings but are linked to systems of inequity and injustice. Through transformative learning people come to understand how aspects of these systems, whether the capitalist economy, government, media, raced and gendered stereotypes, or globalized western culture, benefit a few dominant people and exploit, exclude, or marginalize the rest. Because these systems and their influences on adults' experiences are often invisible or taken for granted as inevitable and unchangeable, adults themselves often unknowingly support their power by accepting these structures and acting in them according to their rules. By exposure to each other's different life stories illustrating the shared systemic repressions that they have experienced, and with help in challenging particular systems contributing to problems in their work lives, education, family, and other spheres of experience, learners together develop new ways of seeing reality.

This critical transformation is described as socially and politically emancipatory, because in the process adults free themselves from existing systems by learning how to recognize their repressiveness. Brookfield (2001) explains:

> A critical theory of adult learning should have at its core an understanding of how adults learn to recognize the predominance of ideology in their everyday thoughts and actions and in the institutions of civil society. It should also illuminate how adults learn to challenge ideology that serves the interests of the few against the well-being of the many. Such a theory is inevitably a theory of social and political learning. It studies the systems and forces that shape adults' lives and oppose adults' attempts to challenge ideology, recognize hegemony, and unmask power. (p. 20)

As excitement with these new insights grows and people support one another in the empowering and liberating experience of transformation through truly critical reflection, motivation builds to take action. These approaches celebrate praxis, the dialectic of critical reflection with socially transformative action taken in changing everyday habits and interactions, collective resistance, and construction of new possibilities. The nature of this action-reflection dialectic is somewhat informed by theories presented in the following section, but its fundamental political commitment must be preserved from dilution.

WHAT ARE THE CONNECTIONS BETWEEN LEARNING AND DOING, LEARNER AND CONTEXT?

Many adults claim that they learn best through "doing" in a particular environment, as when a newcomer to a workplace rapidly develops all the technical skills and cultural know-how needed to function in that organization, almost without thinking about them, through immersion. Given specific tasks to perform using the tools at hand, surrounded by people constantly demonstrating the accepted procedures in this place, testing out ways of interacting, trying, erring, hearing others' tips and explanations, correcting, gradually building social networks—learning *in situ* is an embodied experience that depends upon context but also interweaves the learner's growing identity. Elizabeth McIsaac (2000), a researcher of indigenous knowledge, shares people's stories about how experiential learning was rooted in the land and the relationship with a kinship mentor: "I went with my father, when he was going hunting. I didn't realize I was being taught, but I learned it by seeing it and doing it without really feeling like I was learning" (McIsaac, 2000, p. 95). In the process of this direct knowing, a communion is entered, what Marlene Castellano (2000) describes as congruence between inner and outer reality. People explore inner space as well as the physical world, entering deeply into the inner being of the mind and seeking to be fully connected with the outer world. Thus, experiential learning involves becoming fully aware sensually to one's reality, acutely attuned emotionally, physically and intuitively to interpret all its complexities—a holistic knowledge.

In the tradition of westernized adult education, David Boud and David Walker (1991) introduced a model of experiential learning similar to the mental reflection-based model of David Kolb's, with two main enrichments. First, they acknowledged that specific contexts shape an individual's experience in different ways. Second, they were interested in how differences among individuals—particularly their past histories, learning strategies, and emotions—influence how a person interacts with the environment. For Boud and Walker, the extent of our learning corresponds to the way we *prepare* for an experience, the *noticing and intervening* of our participation in the actual experience, and the processes we use to recall and *reevaluate* an experience, attending to feelings the experience provoked. In preparation we examine the opportunities of the milieu and form particular intentions. We also bring certain skills and strategies of observation and meaning-making, as well as personal histories of past experience.

During a particular experience we each notice and intervene with different elements of the milieu depending on our individual predispositions. We balance our observations with awareness of our own reactions. We choose ways to participate in the activity, to name the learning process, to respond to different events, and to deal with the unexpected—all by reflecting in action. Afterwards we recall and reevaluate our experiences through four processes. *Association* is relating new information to familiar concepts. *Integration* is seeking connection between the new and the old. *Appropriation* is personalizing the new knowledge to make it our own, and *validation* is determining the authenticity of our new ideas and the feelings of the experience. Notice that this model dwells especially on feelings, claiming that negative feelings, if not attended to, can block potential learning in the experience. Boud and his associates also show the importance of preparation or readiness the learner brings to the experience, and the significance of the particular context in which the learner is acting.

But much of our most significant experiential learning is

not easily compartmentalized into separate occasions and contexts that are prepared for, entered, then debriefed through a
reflective evaluation. Autobiography—a process of purposeful
reflection on our life stories to find meaning, weaving together
many forms and occasions of our memoried experience—is a
form of experiential learning championed by adult educators
such as Pierre Dominicé (2000), Nod Miller (2000), and Linden
West (1996, 2001). Through autobiography, a person's sense of
self interacting with context becomes more apparent, for the
individual watches and listens to the self acting in various contexts over periods of time. In adult education, West (1996) has
shown how the act of creating an autobiography helps people
develop a cohesive and resilient self, which he argues is critical
in this age of fragmentation, anxiety, and crisis. In a broader
sense, autobiographical reflection helps learners understand
patterns of their changing environments—social, cultural, economic, political—and their own transitions and responses to
these. In his book *Learning from Our Lives* (2000), Pierre
Dominicé calls this process of reflecting on one's history of experiences in contexts of home, schooling, work, and community
an educational biography. The main learning is making meaning of one's life, which helps adults develop confidence and self-
direction for future learning, and interpreting one's never-end-
ing struggle for identity. Dominicé calls this "becoming more
like ourselves":

> The difficult process of becoming oneself implies confronting, in
> one's life project and learning experiences, the values and models
> acquired from family, school and social life. (p. 73).

> We reconstruct what we already have. We adjust our needs to the
> demands of the context before us and can choose the context
> according to our demand . . . We are not educated until we edu-
> cate ourselves. (p. 80)

The important point is that the learning process knits us
into the activities, objects, and people of the different lifeworlds
or contexts through which we move as learners. As we explore,
experiment, err, and adjust to the demands of these environ-

ments, knowledge becomes embodied and strongly linked to elements of context. Some learning may become tacit knowledge—things we believe, know, or can do perhaps even without conscious awareness. Socio-cultural theorists might argue that we only perform particular actions competently or with flow in certain contexts: imagine trying to cook in someone else's kitchen, for example. Through reflection on how different contexts influence our experiential learning, we may make sense of our actions, piece together an identity, or jolt ourselves into changing certain habitual behaviors and thinking.

But this presumes the learner is separated from environment, that context is a container in which the learner floats. Those who question this separation and challenge the importance placed on reflection and meaning-making[2] suggest a slightly different conception: a complete interrelation of person and community in the learning process. This brings another question into focus.

HOW IS EXPERIENTIAL LEARNING INTERRELATED WITH COMMUNITIES OF PRACTICE?

One problem with explaining experiential learning in ways explained in the preceding sections—as a straightforward matter of individuals reflecting carefully and even critically upon their experiences—is that we are embedded so thoroughly in our cultures that we may not be able to fully distance our thinking from our own experiences. John Garrick (1999), for example, reminds us that what we imagine to be our experience is in fact created by the particular discourses[3] comprising a situation. These discourses shape how we perceive what Schön called routine and nonroutine problems, which we approach and reflect upon differently. For example, in a teaching discourse of classroom control, learners who resist the instructor's directions or act in ways that disrupt order may be labeled as problems that must be disciplined to restore order. In the same situation, a different teaching discourse of authentic dialogue might frame the resistance as an important refusal of coercive power and as an expression of new ideas that disturb prevailing myths. Therefore, an important dynamic to consider in those occasions that we consider to be learning experiences, is how the processes of our cultural images, behavioral norms, language, and values—in which we are saturated—create our perceptions. These processes shape what we believe counts as an experience, how we interpret the experience, and what knowledge we consider worthy learning in the experience.

For situative theorists, knowing and learning are defined as engaging in changing processes of human participation in a particular community of practice. A community of practice is any group of individuals who work together for a period, developing particular ways of doing things and talking about things that their members come to learn—such as a sports team, a workplace department or project group, a class, a club, or a family. In the context of the workplace, Jeff Gold and colleagues (2000) of the Leeds Business School emphasize how the language in a community of practice determines what is considered good and right in that community and what counts as truth and reality. This phenomenon is most evident in the community's stories. These stories are value-saturated and function as a reflective infrastructure to make sense of what is taking place. They not only provide a resource for everyday talk but also, more importantly, preserve the community from outside disturbances (which can be named as negative, or as countering the community's best interests). Through dozens of direct and indirect exchanges with others throughout a single day, individuals adopt various positions and identities, adapt their behavior, choose new action, and contribute to the ongoing network of meanings and collective action. The community itself learns, write Gold and his colleagues, by improvising new practices through these networks in response to a problem or difficulty.

A study of a prominent flute manufacturing plant (Cook & Yanow, 1993) showed that group learning is as much about *preservation* of distinct practices as about innovation. The community of practice functioned and inaugurated new members, even experts from another firm, through a largely tacit, hand-to-hand process. As each flute was passed to the next craftsperson to work on, comments focused on the "right feel" of the flute (for this firm) to perfect its build or correct an "odd feel" in its workings. This process invoked learning among the whole community of practice: while the individual was being initiated the community was learning to adapt to the newcomer's idiosyncracies while preserving its own identity. An individual cannot be considered separately from the configuration. Every practical judgment made amidst everyday "hot action" (Beckett & Hager, 2000) is embedded in the sorts of activity and talk and one-to-one interactions that are allowed and tacitly understood in a particular community of practice. Exactly how this relational learning occurs invites our next question.

HOW ARE SOCIAL RELATIONSHIPS INVOLVED IN EXPERIENTIAL LEARNING?

Some people, argues Dorothy MacKeracher (1996), prefer to learn through relationships while others prefer more autonomous, self-directed modes of experiential learning. Relational learners may seek conversation to help spark or clarify their ideas. They may like to experiment or observe processes in company with others. People also rely on their relational experiences to connect with the experiences of others, to make sense of different viewpoints. Danielle Flannery (2000) summarizes research on women's learning in community groups, work organizations, and study circles revealing similar findings: that the women studied all preferred learning in supportive, collaborative relationships—testing one's stories and perceptions with others, obtaining advice from others' personal experiences, seeking connection with others, and relying on a wide circle for sympathetic hearing and confidence bolstering.[4] Literature has also accumulated suggesting that women's learning is bound up with their development of identity and self-esteem, which occurs through their relational experiences (Caffarella & Olson, 1993).

Joke Vandenabeele and Danny Wildemeersch (2000) present a model of social learning based on individuals changing

by being exposed to different configurations—people holding
different views—in their relationships. They applied the model
in studies of how people learn public issues experientially, such
as participating in political debates or developing new attitudes
about sustainable development. Their model shows how an individual's private learning, that is, a person's internal world
of perceptions and meanings about a particular public issue,
changes through social relationships. Each community in which
an individual participates has its own public meanings and its
own identity or way of acting in the issue. A person participates
in a given community in a specific way, voicing particular opinions and acting/responding according to the specific relationships she or he interacts with. All of these interactions contribute to shaping the community. Meanwhile, the person, too, is
shaped by these interactions, especially when the person is
forced to confront someone bearing different meanings of reality. As individuals interact across different communities, they
bring meanings from one group to another, in turn challenging
the new group's definitions of reality. Always there is tension
between the individual's beliefs and societal meanings. Neither
is determined completely by the other, and both are always
shifting through the interactions in relationships. But key to
both the individual and societal learning is "a continuing process of dialogue and co-operation with people located in other
configurations . . . It is a continuous, never ending process of
making unexpected connections between different configurations" (Vandenabeele & Wildemeersch, 2000, pp. 128–129).

This may be one reason why dialogue is closely linked with
experiential learning. We have seen how, through conversation,
people both affirm their experiences and challenge them. We
dialogue to connect with, learn from, or challenge the different
experiences and interpretations shared by others. We come together through conversation to plan, make sense of, celebrate,
and grieve over experiences we have shared together. Through
dialogue we retell experience stories that build solidarity or help
us work through conflict. Pierre Dominicé shows that important
learning occurs in the act of putting words to one's life stories.
In his method, people listen to and discuss oral narratives, and

experiment with several versions of their own experience story themselves—all towards finding meaning, links to larger forces, and future direction in these experiences. The important foundation for dialogue and relational learning in general is to care sufficiently about understanding each other's differences. Given widespread agreement with this statement, the persistence of ignorance and discrimination based on the precise lack of this understanding is surprising. We therefore are compelled to question again.

HOW ARE CULTURE AND DIVERSITY INTERCONNECTED WITH EXPERIENTIAL LEARNING?

Much writing in adult education has challenged the representation of experiential learning apart from the multiple dimensions of identification and power constituting our experiences: gender, race, class, sexual orientation, physical and mental abilities, religious ties, ethnicity, age, and so on. *Women as Learners* (Hayes, Flannery, with Brooks, Tisdell, & Hugo, 2000) demonstrates how profoundly gender, for example, shapes individuals' experience, including their understandings of learning, opportunities, achievements, and self-images. Feminist educators have argued that women often have difficulty accessing informal learning opportunities in institutions, job sites, and networks dominated by powerful social and economic groups (Probert, 1999). Women's experiential knowledge through childcare and relationships continues to be undervalued, and the language in which they voice their experiences and knowledge may be dismissed in some groups.

But gender cannot be considered apart from other dimensions of diversity in experiential learning. Exclusion and persecution are experienced by individuals stereotyped through race, sexuality, class, and other categories. Nor can gendered experiences be generalized, easily compared, or presumed shared across other dimensions. Groups identified by race, sexual, or ethnic origins are not homogeneous. They often contain many subgroups, often intermingled in complex ways that defy classification. Individuals affiliate with subgroups in unpredictable ways. They may or may not construct their experiences and identities according to skin colour, nation of origin, neighborhood, or socially gendered norms. Groups also may form along certain lines of difference to protest practices that marginalize them or to protect their rights from social or economic oppression. Many of these groups evolve a unique culture, adopting Nicky Solomon's (2001) definition of culture: "a way of life . . . how people group and identify themselves, that is the social human bonds, shared goals, belief systems and values that connect people . . . as they relate to each other and make meaning of their lives" (p. 41).

Liberal notions of multiculturalism seek simply to allow expression of these different cultural forms, without questioning the power relations that distribute resources and privileges unequally among them. Meanwhile diversity continues to be undervalued, misunderstood, and subtly excluded from the dominant narratives and norms used to describe and assess experiences, both in educational and broader social settings. For example, the conventional masculine/feminine categories of gender and sex restrict human expression of experience and learning to a narrow set of characteristics and practices. Lesbian, gay, transgendered, and bisexual experiences are too often named deviant, criminal, or not named at all. Meanwhile the many natural blurrings between rigid categories that constitute the gendered experiences of most human beings are often secret sources of confusion. Labels such as at-risk, low-income, working class, and ethnic references (i.e., Italian-American, Chinese-Canadian) obscure the complex and often contradictory learning experiences of individuals who live multiple and often hybrid identities across many cultural affiliations. Literary stories of such experiences like those collected by Lisa Baumgartner and Sharan Merriam (2000) reveal with luminous poignancy those rich dimensions of learning that our academic language struggles to describe.

People's experiential learning is textured by their struggles to fit in with or fight dominant cultural norms; to withstand discrimination, cruel treatment, and alienation; to create alternate identity models besides the prevalent negative images ascribed to particular racial, ethnic, or sexual identities; to break free of stereotyped expectations of their behavior patterns, capabilities, and interests; or to struggle for basic rights. Literature addressing Afrocentricity (Collins, 1990) and indigenous knowledge (Graveline, 1998) have also argued that western models of learning, with their assumptions of individualized self-direction and rational enlightenment, are fundamentally incongruent with other worldviews whose holistic and embodied cosmologies, ontologies, epistemologies, and axiologies shape alternate experiences and learning.[5] Patricia Hill Collins (1990) argues that black people not only share a common experience of oppression shaping their knowledge, but a distinctive way of knowing. Her Africentric feminist perspective of experiential learning describes this as emphasizing personal, emotional, and spiritual meanings of experience, strongly influenced by storytelling and dialogue in community, and by African-centered collective identity.

An important first step to understanding culture and identity in experiential learning is to interrogate the philosophy and norms underpinning our own educational practice. Writing our own life narratives can provide a space to begin examining how our various communities, power relations, identities, cultural affiliations, and social interactions have constructed our actions in particular ways that defy any definition of "normal" experience. Then we can examine our personal narratives of teaching and learning interactions to ask:

- What norms and discourses of learning, experience, and education are apparent in our practices that potentially repress individuals?
- How do these norms potentially marginalize or distort perspectives and values of particular people?
- What experiences of oppression are rendered invisible by the materials, instructional activities, and facilitation approaches we use?
- In what ways do we still presume sameness among people?

- Who enjoys (unacknowledged) privilege through our pedagogies?
- What knowledge counts most in the ways we emphasize and reward certain ideas and skills?
- What knowledge becomes erased or undervalued in our work with adult learners?

Critical writers emphasize that groups should actively resist the pressure to conform to dominant norms of experience and learning, which tend to be founded on white, middle-class, midlife values. These often ignore or negate the approaches and values held by many other groups. bell hooks (1994), for example, calls for educators to "transgress" the acceptable: first recognize one's own cultural identity and assumptions about culture and difference; critically evaluate the dominant cultural norms and discourses of the educational setting as these repress others; then actively disrupt the taken-for-granted norms and the natural assumptions. For example, educators should critically analyse ideals of harmony, trust, safety, sociality, and connectedness that are frequently advocated for facilitating experiential learning. Safe environments are often only so for white, middle-class participants. Resistance or conflict in learning situations is often suppressed or treated as a problem requiring resolution, as if its perpetrators are difficult learners. Thus those who are different are represented as if they are deficient and need fixing. Perhaps just as repressively, they are sometimes treated as exotic unheard voices that need to be included (that is, domesticated) in ways that leave intact the dominant authorities.

Elizabeth Tisdell (1995) outlines ways of understanding differences without colonizing them, by examining and critiquing the structured power relations and forms of resistance that unfold among a learning community. Tisdell also suggests approaches for creating more broadly inclusive learning environments and educational practices. Solomon (2001) suggests that "it may help to consider who is different to whom, how they are different and who identifies them as different . . . It is problematic to examine difference within a presumption of commonalty, where differences are categorized in relation to a common standard. Perhaps a way forward is to consider that working with difference challenges our understanding of these categories by the very nature of who we think we are" (p. 49). Our senses of personal identity are obviously entwined with our experiences of being "different" from others. Within these experiences, questions about the configuration of our bodies loom large.

WHERE IS THE BODY IN EXPERIENTIAL LEARNING?

Recently, educators have expressed concern for disembodiment in adult education through a concentration on talk and reflection, even in so-called experience-based learning (Chapman, 1996). Studies on *embodied knowing* and "somatic knowledge" (knowledge of the body and knowledge gained through the body) are attracting growing academic and practitioner interest. Three concerns in particular can be identified in this writing. The first is a fear that the body's sensations, stresses, and development all but disappear in educational writing and practice. The result is people either unaware of their body's processes and the impacts on their intellectual processes, or dismissing their physical experiences as irrelevant in learning, or even shameful. This is not only a health issue, but a diminishing of personhood as a whole being, valued and accommodated in all its unique physical, emotional, and sexual capabilities. Aging bodies in particular, among adult learners, risk being pathologized as barriers rather than productive sites for experiential learning.

The second concern, related to the first, is for the potential erasure or invisibility of knowledge centered in the body or generated through the body's interactions with the world. This knowledge is typically undervalued or just not apparent in a world attuned to intellective knowledge. Thus sexual experience and growth may be utterly excised from discussions of experiential learning. Piano players or potters may be labeled as technicians, less important in their contributions than composers or painters. Clerical workers' craft knowledge, physical, and emotional labor may be unacknowledged until its loss alerts an organization to its importance. Physical and associated emotional expression is carefully restricted to particular arenas of sports, dance, carnival, or intimate private spaces.

Third, academic alarm has centered on the ways people participate in disciplining their own bodies according to restrictive and sometimes destructive norms. Following Foucault, writers have shown how discourses inscribe our bodies not through authoritarian constraints, but through our own desires. People willingly decorate or demean, constrict, punish, and ignore parts of their bodies in learning projects that pursue (or sometimes protest) culturally sanctioned images of beauty, health, or status.

Educational responses that are advocated tend to concentrate on raising personal and cultural bodily awareness, reincorporating the body into learning activities and theories, and enabling human beings to expand and value bodily experiences and knowledge. Bodily awareness includes both theoretical analysis and pedagogical practice. The former examines ways that the body is socially molded, physically trained, culturally disciplined, and sexually repressed and distorted. The latter may borrow exercises from dance, theatre, or yoga to enhance sensual awareness and raise physical consciousness of one's body surfaces and interactions in space with other objects, or open new possibilities of experience available through the body—ecstacy, pain, intimacy, pleasure, connection, and flow. Some urge greater emphasis in adult education on integrating cognition and emotion, holding discussions that honor bodily experiences and put them into language, examining meanings or judgments we give to these experience, or encouraging learners to critically examine the social inscriptions marked upon their bodies (Grosz, 1994).

All of these perspectives may describe themselves as ecological to the extent that they advocate for a return to wholeness in understanding and facilitating adults' experiential learning. However, those writers on learning aligning themselves with complexity or enaction theories (such as Varela et al., 1991), which are characterized as "ecological" theorists here, go even further in their considerations of the body. For FranciscoVarela,[6] for example, there is no separation of the body from concepts and values, or separation of the person as subject from objects, including knowledge. His understanding of cognition as bringing forth a world in action has been hailed as a vision of a fully embodied knowledge.

There is, however, a danger in the renewed academic focus on bodily knowledge in contemporary environments infused with human capital theory, where learning is so often subordinated to the logic of exchange. An example is the objective uttered frequently by organizational theorists of drawing forth or harvesting "tacit knowledge" embedded in human bodies and action to increase performance (Nonaka & Takeushi, 1995). This appropriation and commodification of embodied knowledge is not confined to corporate or private interests. Academics and educators must also be reflexively aware of our own purposes for wanting to explore, make explicit, and expand the body's engagement in experiential learning. Evidently within questions of the body's involvement in experiential learning, desire functions as an important nexus of cultural influence and personal agency in motivating action and producing meaning.

HOW DO OUR DESIRES CONFIGURE OUR EXPERIENTIAL LEARNING?

Sharon Todd (1997), introducing *Learning Desire,* asks, How do we understand and engage desire? How are conflicting desires at the heart of our learning/teaching encounters? Desire is not a straightforward lack of something compelling us to seek it. It can be understood in multiple ways. First, desire may be both learned and implicated in the learning process. We may not have any desire to know something about a particular field of study until, perhaps, we become involved in a project where we begin to experience that field. As we learn a little, at the edges so to speak, we may begin to develop or *learn* a desire to learn more. The general question is, How did we learn to desire the knowledge that we currently pursue in our learning endeavors?

Second, the location and direction of desire are more complex than traditional psychological notions of innate human needs imply. Derek Briton (1997) suggests that the object of our desire (for knowledge) both attracts and repels us, and is sometimes situated at the very heart of ourselves. As well, our object of desire is often uncannily transformed into something we hate. For example, we may feel compelled to know something which, when we finally understand it fully, is too horrible to contemplate—or perhaps so mundane that we disdain it with contempt. Third, as Todd (1997) observes, "There are conflicting desires at the heart of the pedagogical encounter itself between what is said (what we say we want) and how we say it (the affective and psychical investments embedded therein; what is left unsaid)" (p. 7). So with respect to understanding experiential learning, psychoanalytic theorists ask, What are these dynamics of longing? How do desires configure limits as well as possibilities for individuals' participation in new knowledge?

Jacques Lacan's (1978) explanation of the psychic dynamics of longing and learning have become influential in learning theory. Lacan proposed three registers in which our psychic world meets the external world. The Imaginary is a preverbal register of ideals using a visual logic, springing from a childhood understanding of itself as a mirror image, undifferentiated from and desiring to complete its mother. The Symbolic register is the language and laws of culture, of which the child becomes part. Here the individual experiences conflicts between the limits of legitimate vocabulary in the Symbolic register, with the desires and images experienced in the Imaginary register. The Real register is a central sense of lack that drives the individual but cannot be understood by the conscious mind. Slavoj Zizek (1991) explains that we cover over this Real lack of ours, encountering it only in traumatic dreams in which "our common everyday reality, the reality of the social universe in which we assume our roles of kind-hearted, decent people, turns out to be an illusion that rests on certain repression, on overlooking the [R]eal of our desire. This social reality is then nothing but a fragile, symbolic cobweb that can at any moment be torn aside by an intrusion of the [R]eal" (p. 17). Although we may not consciously understand this desire, we sense its presence, and so project it onto things that we desperately seek, believing that in attaining them we can satisfy this central lack.

Mark Bracher (1993) explains that our subjectivity or self is, in essence, these projections of desire to have some other things or be some other things, or to have others possess us or desire us. Through the process of becoming social and appropriating our culture's language, we learn to represent or adapt some of these projections in particular language. We also learn which of these desires are allowed or forbidden by our culture. In terms of experiential learning, Lacanian theory portrays human individuals at a psychic level as essentially suffering— amidst contradictory desires, repressed desires, and terror at confronting the Real desire that we sense is lurking beneath our safe constructions of reality and our selves. Yet we do not suffer in isolated cells, for clearly our memories of our own experiences reveal a rich fabric of connections and interactions that have textured our learning. We know that our desires, thoughts, and movements are entwined with others' in dynamic systems, leading us to the next question.

HOW IS LEARNING PART OF COMPLEX SYSTEMS?

Many educationists have adapted the principles of complex adaptive systems to understand experiential learning and propose roles for educators in an ecological framework. William Doll (1993), working from the ideas of Ira Prigogine (1997), suggests a new, more fluid and emergent way to develop curriculum and classroom practice. Irene Karpiak (2000) develops a model for higher education teaching based on complexity theory. And in Canada, Brent Davis and Dennis Sumara (1997) with Rebecca Luce-Kapler (2000) have created teaching ideas, research approaches, and curriculum theory applying complexity theory to what they now call ecological learning.

For a brief overview of some principles underlying all of this work, a good starting place is the complex adaptive system. A person is a whole system, made up of many biological (digestive, neuro-muscular, etc.), sensory, mental, and emotional systems. These systems in turn are made up of parts, like organs, which are complete systems in themselves. But a person is also a part of other systems: family systems and social systems, which in turn are nested in national systems, which are part of even larger forces like global market systems. A system is *self-modifying*—sensitive and responding to changes within it and around it—in constant dialogue with its environment. Its many components are always alive, always interacting creatively with parts directly around them. These interactions form patterns all by themselves—they do not organize according to some sort of externally imposed blueprint—so we say that such systems are *self-organizing*.

The outcome of all these dynamic interactions of a system's parts is *unpredictable*. So many things are going on all at once that the system is quite literally impossible to understand by breaking it down and studying these parts, or by trying to reduce it to a series of causes and effects. Thus everything from a weather system to an economic system to a human being is described as a *complex* system, rather than simply a complicated one with a mechanical, predictable system of parts, such as a car or a coffee-maker. A complex system is never stable or fixed, but always *adapting* in unpredictable ways. The key to a healthy system—able to adapt creatively to changing conditions—is *diversity* among its parts. A human body, for example, relies on highly specialized subsystems that not only each respond to different circumstances and different needs, but also have learned to cohabitate and communicate with one another. One final interesting characteristic of many complex adaptive systems is *self-similarity* in its patterns. A large fern, for example, exactly resembles the structures of one branch of the fern, and one single leaf of the branch. Thus, a system can be studied by looking closely at one part as well as at the whole body of relationships among parts.

All complex adaptive systems learn—where learning is defined as transformation that expands a learner's potential range of action. Research on HIV-AIDs systems, for example, demonstrates that the immune system remembers, forgets, recognizes, hypothesizes, errors, adapts, and thus learns (Davis, Sumara, & Luce-Kapler, 2000). Forests and other ecosystems, weather systems, human communities, and market systems all learn. Part of this learning is the continuous creation of alternate actions and responses to changing situations, undertaken by the system's parts. More sudden transformation can occur in response to a major shock to the system, throwing it into *disequilibrium*. Computer-generated images of systems undergoing disequilibrium show that they go through a phase of swinging between extremes, before self-organizing gradually into a new pattern or identity that can continue cohabiting with and adapting to the other systems in its environment. After the episode the system resumes its continuous improvisation, although more resilient and more flexible to learn its way through anomalies it encounters. Learning, then, does not simply occur within the worlds of isolated individuals, although human beings do function as whole systems that learn, adapt, organize, and transform themselves as distinct identities. But human beings also are part of larger systems that learn, adapt, organize, and transform themselves as distinct identities. As parts of these continuously learning larger systems, humans themselves bear characteristics of larger patterns, larger identities—a little like the single fern leaf resembling the whole fern plant. The difference is that humans participate in many complex learning systems at once.

But critics point out that a complex system can continuously learn and adapt itself very effectively for dysfunctional, inequitable, oppressive, destructive, even evil purposes. So how can individual parts of the system, such as humans in a certain social system, learn in ways that may change the system in more generative, democratic, healthy directions? And how is learning diffused through a system, or translated across systems?

HOW DOES KNOWLEDGE DEVELOPED THROUGH EXPERIENCE TRANSFER TO OTHER SITUATIONS?

Overly strict interpretations of knowledge transfer have led some to argue that people do not carry knowledge and skill learned in one context to another—a notion that defies common-sense observation. A strict psychological constructivist view tends to define transfer of learning as unassisted and spontaneous, which is unrealistic. A strict situative view maintains that each different context evokes different knowings through very different demands of participation. What is learned in one site is therefore not portable, but is transformed and reinvented when applied to the tasks, interactions, and cultural dynamics of another. However, constructivist learning theorists have argued that situative claims overstate the insistence that knowledge is context-dependent (Anderson, Reder, & Simon, 1996, p. 5). They assert that the extent to which learning is tightly bound to context depends on the kind of knowledge being acquired and the ways the material is engaged.

Thus, many cognitive learning theorists agree cautiously that transfer is a legitimate construct. The constructivist theorists may claim that what is truly important in learning is "what cognitive processes a problem evokes, and not what real-world trappings it might have" (Anderson et al., 1996, p. 9). Situative theorists may quibble, as Anna Sfard (1998) explains, that the notion of knowledge transfer implies carrying knowledge across contextual boundaries that don't exist: when neither knowledge nor context is viewed as clearly delineated areas, "there are no definite boundaries to be crossed" (p. 9). Organizational learning theorists have suggested a combination of constructivist and situative explanations for knowledge transfer. These writers often distinguish tacit knowledge that is implicit and embodied in our actions, from so-called explicit knowledge that people can consciously articulate to others. Transfer, then, supposedly happens through socialization (tacit knowledge of one person or group is transferred to others as tacit knowledge), externalization (tacit to explicit), combination (explicit to explicit), and internalization (explicit to tacit) (Nonaka & Takeushi, 1995). The distinction drawn here between conscious and unconscious, or embodied and spoken knowledge, tends to ignore the messy blendings among these in everyday experiential learning.

In practice, educators who believe that knowledge is in fact learned and then transferred or applied to new contexts might draw from recommendations advanced by different groups. Tacit knowledge might be applied more expansively by individuals and groups by ensuring that it gets recognized, demonstrated, shared, and somehow put into language. Constructivists suggest that transfer of learning is increased when learners have multiple concrete examples and situations, sufficient practice, instruction in transferable elements of skills being learned, and assistance in new contexts to adapt and apply previously learned knowledge and skills. They also suggest the importance of individual capacity to be self-directed in learning from experience, analysing experiential learning, developing strategies, and monitoring one's own learning. Situative theories imply that people's use of new skills in unfamiliar contexts is assisted by contextual features such as supervisor support, supportive peers and group norms, authentic opportunities to use new skills, and positive personal outcomes. But it is wise to remember that the concept of transfer has very little utility in perspectives that do not regard the individual as the site of knowledge. Ecological and some critical perspectives, for example, regard learning as fluid and continuously invented or circulating in networks of action, certainly not "transferred" from one fixed space to another.

CONCLUSION

The questions about experiential learning presented in this chapter are intended to be representative, not exhaustive, showing dimensions that may be of most interest to educators. The chapter opened with a caveat that selected models and suggestions described here need to be read critically. I have one other caution. The questions presented in this chapter all use the terms *experiential learning* and *learning* without distinguishing important differences in the kinds of learning that are unfolding. Clearly there are many forms of knowledge enmeshed with experiential learning that are worth setting apart to analyse, and many writers have done so (Billett, 2001; Jarvinen, 1998; MacKeracher, 1996; Malinen, 2000; Mezirow, 1991). Some have divided these into three clusters ranging from learning technical skills or concepts and practical know-how; to developing social/relational ability, attitudes, emotional and personal knowledge; to experiencing powerful challenges to our ways of thinking and acting that cause dramatic change. But the debates are far from reaching conclusions about just how different these knowledges are, whether they are separated, where they exist (in a person's head? in a social group?), how they develop, and what evidence they show.

As important as these issues are, however, this chapter's discussion would be distorted by attempts to link categories of knowledge with specific dimensions of experiential learning. In some cases particular kinds of knowledge are clearly implied, but the reader is left to imagine personal contexts of experiential learning where a particular explanation may have most relevancy. For similar reasons, discussion of specific questions here has not sufficiently addressed deep divisions between educators and theorists related to the nature of the learning process, the relation of a learner to the learning context, and pedagogical purposes within experiential learning. These debates are taken up in the following chapter.

NOTES

1. For a clear and thorough explanation of both Mezirow's theory and his many critics, as well as empirical studies applying the theory of transformative learning to various contexts of adult experience, consult the monograph *The Theory and Practice of Transformative Learning* by Edward Taylor (1998).
2. Writers addressing embodied knowing do so from a wide range of perspectives, including McIsaac, Castellano, and others explaining

indigenous knowledge, Buddhist-influenced writers such as Varela (1989) and Africentric writers (i.e., Collins, 1990).

3. A discourse is system of cultural practices, norms, values, and words that reinforce particular beliefs and behaviors, framing life in a particular way. A particular discourse endorses some ways of acting as normal or desirable, depicts others as bad or irrational, and completely ignores still others by not naming them.

4. Critiques have shown that generalizing any conception of "women's ways" of learning is inaccurate and ignores how preferences for relational learning may be a good deal more related to historical socialization of gender and to cultural characteristics irrespective of gender.

5. Cosmology is one's view of the reality in the universe, including dimensions of time, space, nature, and the position of humankind. Ontology is how one views the nature of living and nonanimate beings in the universe. Epistemology is one's perspective of knowledge: what knowledge is, and how people come to know their worlds. Axiology is one's morality, including what one distinguishes as good or bad.

6. Important to note is Varela's influence by Buddhist practices of mindfulness and the education of desire, which he incorporated into his theories of cognition and enaction. Buddhist meditation, Varela maintained, provides a key to access experience.

CHAPTER 4

Critiques and Debates

Jonathan Grossman (1999) argues that experiential learning has now become both a philosophy and a method. As philosophy, it asserts that learning takes place in the experience of everyday life and that therefore all people have knowledge and expertise. As method, it can be "reduced to particular techniques [that are] always ideologically and politically framed . . . used in the service of diametrically opposed interests" (p. 213). The many critiques of experiential learning tend to split along these two lines. Those focusing on philosophy are grouped below into a selection of prominent theoretical debates of experiential learning itself. These tend to center on the nature of self, context, mind, and body in experiential learning. The second part of this chapter is devoted to pedagogical debates. These are limited here to the issue of assessing experiential learning, the charge that educating through experiential learning is an act of colonization, and the rebuttal that without (critical) educational intervention, oppressive social orders simply reproduce themselves. This pedagogical section ends with a brief introduction to long-standing debates about what should be the purpose of experiential learning.

THEORETICAL DEBATES

In this book, experiential learning is stretched to wider reaches than may typically be considered part of the field of adult education. Fields such as psychoanalysis, ecology, feminism, cultural studies, and the growing literature about working knowledge and communities of practice can enrich our under-standings of learning through experience. They help us analyse more critically the rapidly changing domains (such as virtual fields) and policies affecting experiential learning. They also contribute important new insights about possible roles and forms of pedagogical intervention for educators. But perspec-tives raised in these fields often appear to attack one another's basic beliefs about experiential learning elements, processes, and purposes. Six critiques in particular appear to be most cru-cial in considering the future of experience-based learning:

1. Critique of the educative notion of building a coherent self.

2. Critique of the belief that individuals exist separately from their social contexts.

3. Critique of models representing experience as concrete.

4. Critique of educative emphasis on cognitive reflection in ex-periential learning.

5. Critique of experimental trial-and-error as useful learning.

6. Critique of the notion that adults are empowered through critical reflection on experience.

Finally, a continuing issue for educators is whether or how to somehow bound the concept of experiential learning before it consumes everything that constitutes life itself. These critiques are presented below in the form of statements that challenge prevailing views, followed by selected arguments in the debates offered by contrasting voices.

The unitary self view is problematic, but still dominates experiential learning.

I suggested in Chapter 1 that our view of what constitutes a self is fundamental in shaping how we understand the nature of experiential learning, but that opinions range widely. The constructivist view considers the individual self a primary actor in knowledge construction, which is cast as a conscious, mentalist process. The learner is assumed to be a stable fixed identity, with transparent access to experience through rational reflection. But so-called postmodern views debunk this self as an illusion, showing that our subjectivity is multiple and always shifting. What we construe as our authentic self having experiences is a story we tell in particular contexts for particular purposes, which can be reshaped by infinite configurations and voices. As we saw in Chapter 3, in our self-storying, rural and urban geographies play with political dynamics, racial issues, gender, and religious ties. Overlap and dissonance among these dynamics mix with the identity choices we make consciously (Loutzenheiser, 2001). Ecologists argue that the boundaries between self and non-self (nature as well as society) are actually more permeable and the flow between them more continuous than we might be prepared to accept.

Psychoanalytic theorist Jacques Lacan (1978) adds useful insights about self as a split subject. Lacan proposes that there is no entity existing as a unified self, as ego psychology would have it. Instead, the subject's identity is split between conscious and unconscious desires that are continually misrecognized. The subject is also split by imaginary illusions sustained in the language or Symbolic register. Lacan proposes that our split subjectivity is evident when we try to think or talk about our experiences. The I (je) doing the enunciating is different and distanced from the me (moi), the object of the talk, the image of a person whose actions-amidst-experience we construct when we reflect from a distance, borrowing from various images and vocabulary available in our cultures. The identity of the I subject has no material existence, and can't talk about itself at the same time as it experiences itself. It is pure drive, seeking identity to fulfill its own lack of a sense of real identity. Kaja Silverman (1992) explains: "it is only in the guise of the moi that the subject takes on a corporeal form, and consequently lays claim to a visual image, and it is only as a refraction of the moi that it is able to desire an object. Identity and desire are so complexly imbricated that neither can be explained without recourse to the other" (p. 6).

Yet others argue compellingly that we need to at least believe that we have an authentic self so we can find purpose in
continuing to struggle and learn. Matthias Finger and José Asún
(2001) agree that identities are split and sliding, but far from
celebrating this understanding they lament the fragmentation
and fluidity of people's selves as a sign of destructive, dead-end
trends in adult education and society in general. For some critical educators such as Paula Allman (2001), the whole point of
learning is to create a coherent, strong self -for only then can
people develop the sense of power they need to struggle against
structural oppression and inequity.

Michelson (1999), however, argues that perpetuation of
unitary self notions brings not just individual agency but also a
form of silent control. According to her, the concept of a self
has evolved from the Enlightenment discovery of an interiorized
subjectivity, where body became the ground for an individual
autonomy (separate from Other) and inner experience became
privatized. In this shift toward privileging self came freedom
and agency, along with the internalization of social control.
Kolb maintained that the modern discovery of a private inner
realm of experience supposedly granted to individuals their
worth, dignity, and liberty to make choices. However, the management of inner experience also became important, to ensure
discipline and regulation of these choices as a bourgeoisie society
arose. Michelson shows how mainstream theories of experiential learning that arose gradually became tied to social relations
of capitalism. As discussed in a later section, this movement to
manage experiential learning poses grave concern for adult educators.

The experiencing learner is *not* separate from the context of experience.

A second area of challenge to reflective constructivism is its
separation of the individual doing the learning and the individual's context. Context involves the social relations and political-
cultural dimensions of the community in which the individual

is caught up, the nature of the task, the web of joint actions in which the individual's choices and behaviors are enmeshed, the vocabulary and cultural beliefs through which the individual makes meaning of the whole situation, and the historical, temporal, and spatial location of the situation. Obviously, these dimensions are crucial to understand how learning unfolds in experience.

In Kolb's model of experiential learning, context is given little consideration. Experience and reflection on experience are portrayed as if this learning exists in what Peter Jarvis (1987) called "splendid isolation." Jarvis suggests that context is constituted partly by the different ways a person interacts with it. He proposes an altered model of experiential learning portraying a person, shaped by a particular sociocultural milieu, moving into and out of various social situations. The person's response might be reflective learning (contemplation, problem solving, or active experimentation), or it might be nonreflective learning (absorbing information, unconsciously internalizing new understandings, or mechanically practicing new skills). A response might even be nonlearning (rejecting learning, too preoccupied to learn, or just interacting mechanically).

Mezirow's theory of transformative learning has been criticized for proposing "a concept of rationality that is essentially ahistorical and decontextualized" (Clark & Wilson, 1991, p. 90). Although his later revisions of his theory recognized learning as situated in a social context, Mezirow, according to Edward Taylor (1998), failed to maintain the connection between the construction of knowledge and the context within which it is interpreted. Boud, Keogh, and Walker (1996), as we saw in Chapter 3, presented context as a significant dimension of learners' immersion in particular events comprising experience. The context presents possibilities from which learners presumably select objects of knowing to interact with. However, they portray context problematically as a static space. The learner is still viewed as fundamentally autonomous from his or her surroundings. The learner moves through context, is in it and affected by it, but the learner's meanings still exist in the mind, and move with the learner from one context to the next. Knowledge is taken to be a substance, a third thing created from the learner's interaction with other actors and objects. Social relations of power exercised through language or cultural practices are not theorized as part of knowledge construction.

Situative theorists criticize this separation of person from context, as if context is a container in which the learner moves, rather than as a web of activity, subjectivities, and language. When context is viewed as this web, elements of experience such as learner, event, action, object, and setting do not appear to be so distinct as the constructivist view sometimes portrays them. Other writers (i.e., Edwards, 1994; Tisdell, 1998) suggest alternative understandings of experience that destabilize unitary identity and social categories, recognize the interplay between body and world, and challenge binaries such as person/context in experiential learning.

Experiential learning models misrepresent experience as concrete and knowable.

Many have critiqued Kolb's assumption that experience is concrete and split from reflection as a sort of dichotomy. With the proliferation of postmodern understandings of the relationship between person, context/culture, and experience, it has become commonplace to assume the discursive production and fluidity of experience. As Michelson (1999) has argued, "experience exceeds rational attempts to bound it, control and rationalize it according to pre-existing social categories and sanctioned uses" (p. 151). From a feminist perspective, Michelson (1996) goes on to observe that emphasis on (critical) reflection depersonalizes the learner as an autonomous rational knowledge-making self, disembodied, rising above the dynamics and contingency of experience. The learning process of reflection presumes that knowledge is extracted and abstracted from experience by the processing mind. This ignores the possibility that all knowledge is constructed within power-laden social processes, that experience and knowledge are mutually determined, and that experience itself is knowledge-driven and cannot be known outside socially available meanings.

Further, argues Michelson (1996), the reflective or constructivist view of development denigrates bodily and intuitive
experience, advocating retreat into the loftier domains of rational thought from which raw experience can be disciplined
and controlled. In her later work she draws attention to experience that is "outrageous and transgressive, experience not easily
reduced to reason and coherence" (Michelson, 1999, p. 145).
She suggests that reflective theories of experiential learning
dominating adult education have actually repressed possibilities
of meaning, knowledge, and identity. Working from the ideas
of Bakhtin, she suggests that the notion of carnival might help
open our theories of experiential learning. Carnival is "a site for
transgressing repressive, overdetermined meanings and creating
knowledge within a wider play of possibilities . . . where we can
welcome the excess of experience and with it, the contingent
quality of both meaning and identity" (p. 145–146).

Her critique of educators is aligned with feminist post-
structuralists such as Mimi Orner (1992) and Elizabeth Tisdell
(1998), who argue that the (distorted) assumption of concrete
experience leads to a mistaken educational orientation of freeing
people from their misconceptions, ideologies, false consciousness, and colonized lifeworlds. Instead, argues Michelson (1999),
educators should be assisting learners to explore the availability
of meanings within our cultures and societies. We cannot deny
people's historically embedded subjectivity or the boundaries of
self. Instead, we should be committed to opening self "to the
transgressive, oppositional Other within our own discourses
and societies" (p. 146). This invites a consideration of experience as invoking conscious, unconscious, and bodily engagements torn between the culturally acceptable and the taboo, the
personally liberating and the repressive. Consider our experience of and responses to advertising implicitly targeting our sexual desires, to overheard comments that hurt our feelings, to
rules that we believe unfair, or to ethical dilemmas forcing us
to choose among unsavory actions. These are everyday learning
experiences. Our reactions depend partly on our uppermost intentions and priorities, our cultural proclivities, our desire to
conform to or resist social norms of an occasion, and our biological and emotional condition at the moment. Experience is

not simply a situation being apprehended but also a positioning of self within that situation, entailing contradictory emotional responses and intuitive perceptions. Meanwhile the experiential moment is simultaneously integrated with our present awareness, past memories, and future speculations. All these dimensions still consider only the interior world. There are multiple levels of experience inviting debate about how we process experience to learn from it, a process which conventional experiential learning theory portrays as conscious mental reflection.

Cognitive reflection is a highly limited mode for experiential learning.

Critics such as Deborah Britzman (1998a) and Dennis Sawada (1991) maintain that the focus of experiential learning theory on cognitive reflection is simplistic and reductionist. First, this focus justifies and emphasizes rational control and mastery, which feminist theorists such as Mechtild Hart (1992) have criticized as a eurocentric, masculinist view of knowledge creation. Second, this reflective constructivist view does not provide any sophisticated understandings of the role of desire in experience and learning, despite its central tenet that a learner's intention guides the inquiry process. Desire is a foundational principle in human experience and knowledge, according to psychoanalytic theories of experience and learning. Third, the focus on rational concept-formation through cognitive reflection sidesteps what Deborah Britzman (1998a) calls the ambivalences and internal vicissitudes bubbling in the unconscious. These, according to Britzman, direct our interpretations and therefore our meaning-making or experience in unpredictable ways.

The emphasis on conscious reflection also ignores or makes invisible those psychic events that are not available to the conscious mind, including the desires and position of the reflecting *I* respective to the reflected-upon *me* being constructed as a container of knowledge. Meanwhile, constructivism does not attend to internal resistances in the learning process, the active "ignore-ances" which Elizabeth Ellsworth (1997) contends are as important in shaping our engagement in experience as attraction to particular objects of knowledge. The view that experience must be processed through reflection clings to binaries drawn between complex blends of doing/learning, implicit/explicit, active/passive, life experience/instructional experience, reflection/action (most notably in Kolb's depiction of perceiving and processing activities conceived as continuums from concrete to abstract engagement). Sawada (1991) shows that understanding reflection as processing reinforces a conduit understanding of learning, relying on an old input-output metaphor of learning where the system becomes input to itself. Furthermore, constructivism falsely presumes a cut universe, where subjects are divided from environment and from their own experiences, and reflection is posited as the great integrator, bridging separations that it creates instead of reorienting us to the whole.

Despite their influence in understanding the processes of experiential learning, psychoanalytic theories have not gone unchallenged. Some question the assumption that the conscious and unconscious are split, and suggest that this sort of binary sets up oppositions that psychoanalytic theory tries to avoid. Donald Vandenberg (1999) questions the definition of consciousness used by Ellsworth, claiming that because perceptual and conceptual consciousness can function independently (such as when driving a car while talking), there is no need to propose an unconscious. From a rational constructivist perspective, Mezirow (1991) acknowledges the perturbations of the unconscious, usually inaccessible to the reflective conscious mind, which often catalyses transformative learning. However he asserts the need to control and subvert, through critical reflection and communicative dialogue, those dysfunctional habits of mind leading to undesirable actions. As rational beings we can overcome our logical contradictions and our unjustified or inarticulable beliefs (Mezirow, 1991) which psychoanalytic theory suggests should be simply accepted as interminable dilemmas. In other words, Mezirow's perspective is that learning is more than just a process of working-through, it is working towards idealized mental frames of reference and towards beliefs that can be validated.

More recently however, Edward Taylor (2001) has sug-

gested that the critical reflection on experience leading to transformative learning is clearly linked to emotions, and should be
understood as an experience linking reason and feeling. Further,
Taylor shows studies based on Mezirow's theory that found
transformative learning occurring *without* rational reflection.
Taylor indicates that nonconscious or "implicit" memory may
play a greater role than has been acknowledged in transformative
experiential learning, and that cognitive reflection may actually
impede the learning process in some cases. Thus, the cognitive
emphasis in some past iterations of transformative experiential
learning may be opening to more expansive understandings.

Experiential learning processes focusing on self-scrutiny ultimately disempower people.

Challengers working from the poststructural ideas of
Michel Foucault have claimed that the focus on critical reflection which dominates the experiential learning discourse is itself
oppressive and disempowering. Foucault (1980) explains that
subjects are regulated through socio-cultural processes (such as
assessments, rewards, and images promoting particular behaviors) that make them knowable and thus controllable. Writers
examining experiential learning in workplaces have drawn from
Foucault's notion of governmentality to criticize the educational
management of experiential learning, and the regulation of subjects doing the experiencing, for organizational goals (Garrick
& Usher, 2000; Harrison, 2000; Usher & Solomon, 1999). For
example, Barbara Townley (1994) has applied Foucault's ideas
to criticize the way workers' experiential learning is governed
by human resource management practices in work organizations. These practices include performance appraisals using normalizing preconstructed standards, constant surveillance of
workers, selection and promotion based on people's learning,
and increasing emphases on workers' self-assessment and con-
fession of their innermost beliefs. Through these practices individuals supposedly internalize the disciplines that regulate their
identities, and thus individual resistance is subverted.

According to Richard Tobias (1999), Foucault's insights reveal that the ideology of individualism embedded in current practices of experiential learning, with its notions of individual choice and individual learning needs, is a social and political construction that shapes particular relations of power. First, the individual is falsely portrayed as a rational, autonomous, self-governing being rather than a subject positioned in a variety of discourses. Second, the focus on lifelong or experiential learning tends to view this individual as a bundle of learning needs, focusing attention on individuals' skill levels in terms of their capacity to serve the system. This tears people from real material and social networks and turns them into objects (of knowledge) and targets (for educational intervention). Thus the system's problems became the individual's learning problems. Concern is then nicely diverted away from social and economic forces that sustain systemic oppression, and focused on "empowering" individuals to learn continuously and serve the system's changing needs.

This shift works to focus people on disciplining their own experiential learning. Foucault (1988) explains how, when subjected to the perpetual surveillance of normalizing practices which classify, measure, and judge them, people begin monitoring and regulating their own behavior to conform with preestablished standards. Eventually they become self-policing, their selves becoming objects of their own critical gaze of measurement and control. Robin Usher and Richard Edwards (1995) criticize confessional educational practices such as journaling, life planning, self-evaluation, portfolios, and counseling, which are commonly associated with experiential learning. These practices, argue Usher and Edwards, require humans to turn upon themselves as objects of scrutiny and knowledge, to construct a stable rational self, to plan and structure the development of this self, and often to do so under the scrutiny of an educator.

The critical argument is that as individuals we are ultimately disempowered. We come to believe that we are isolated individuals each pursuing self-development in lonely, disconnected ways that lack fulfilling purpose. Through technologies of self-governance reinforced by external scrutiny, we grow increasingly anxious, believing ourselves to be continually in need of improvement and terrified of falling behind dominant notions of the ideal self and demands of society. Individual choice and freedom within such practices are illusions. As Foucault (1977) writes, "the power of normalization imposes homogeneity but it individualizes by making it possible to measure gaps, to determine levels, to fix specialties and to render differences" (p. 184). Individuals become constituted by and eventually dependent on the disciplinary power they have internalized and directed upon themselves.

This Foucauldian approach to understanding experience and learning has been criticized for being mechanistic, overdeterministic, and inflexible. It may not sufficiently recognize the dynamics of human agency, and how we exercise some choice in taking up or resisting cultural discourses. However, it illuminates dynamics of power and regulation embedded in our perceptions that we may not recognize. Foucault's argument is that when we as subjects are caught up in and thus controlled by such technologies as reflecting upon experiential learning, our identities are constructed in particular ways, and also our notions of what counts as expertise. This is a homogenizing process, and reduces complex experience to observable, discussable, measurable items. Knowledge becomes conceptualized as a substance to be obtained in a logical sequential way, and experience is cast as raw material to be processed and written down for it to become knowledge, a position that feminists argue to be patriarchal and dehumanizing. If power works in us through cultural systems of classification and knowledge, then our ways of responding to the world (including what we think of as our experiential learning) are textured in ways we may not apprehend.

Experiential learning has limited potential for knowledge production.

In strong contrast to this position a rationalist critique, most notably expressed in some business literature addressing organizational and strategic learning, is that much experiential learning has not demonstrated significant outcomes in terms of overall knowledge development. Furthermore, the notion that all learning is virtuous has been accepted rather uncritically. Trial-and-error processes are not only slow but typically involve a lot of failure in the lessons learned. These do not necessarily yield more effective organizations or more intelligent behavior, and "the same processes that yield experiential wisdom in organizations also produce superstitious learning, competency traps and erroneous inferences" (Levitt & March, 1988, p. 335). The two most celebrated forms of experience in organizational learning literature are continuous experimentation supposedly leading to incremental improvement, and traumatic change supposedly required for transformation and renewal (Leavy, 1998). The former has proven to entrench self-affirming rigidities or dysfunctional practices in organizations, or produce multiple new ideas that cannot be absorbed into practice; the latter invokes destruction and a period of chaos that yield dubious benefit in the long term for betterment either of the organization's or its individuals' well-being (Leavy, 1998). This literature is unapologetically rooted in a belief that learning should advance organizational goals of competition, a position to which many adult educators are ideologically opposed. Nonetheless, it suggests useful critical questions for us about just what is being learned through experiential learning processes, who is benefiting, and whether experiential learning deserves to maintain the idealized status it has acquired in adult education literature.

Experiential learning must be bounded, somehow.

Finally, a continuing issue for educators is whether or how to somehow bound the concept of experiential learning before it embraces everything that constitutes life itself. As noted in Chapter 1, the notion of experiential learning has been applied to such diverse contexts in the field of adult education that there appears to be little concern for definitional consistency or coherence. Experiential learning potentially embraces both educationally directed and nondirected engagements in classrooms, work, community action, as well as ongoing everyday life experiences. Definitional problems continue when we try to disentangle the notion of experiential learning from experiences commonly associated with formal education, such as class discussions, reading and analysis, and reflection. So the question of where to draw the boundaries becomes quickly apparent to educators attempting to define experiential learning. Without boundaries, experiential learning incorporates everything: every living moment, every form of engagement whether more conscious or unconscious, more bodily or reflective, more accidental or intentional, more social or solitary.

The first problem with this no-boundaries view is the practical difficulty of educators trying to take responsibility for all the complexities and fluidity of human life. A second spectre is that the "everything is experiential learning" view collapses all human experience and meaning-making into a learning problem, incidentally inserting the educator as the observer if not active intervener in all human experience. For thoughtful educators, the ethical and political issues in basing practice upon such a position should be obvious. One response to the issue is suggested by Judy Harris (2000): limit pedagogical discussion and intervention in experiential learning to activities or occasions in which an informed adult voluntarily submits to the vulnerable role of learner. More broadly, the issue is approached through a series of debates about the legitimate extent to which pedagogy can be imposed upon people's experiences.

PEDAGOGICAL DEBATES

Issues about pedagogy related to experiential learning include debates about what should be learned in experience-based education, about how such education should be designed, and of course about what role if any the educator should play. Some debates have arisen from direct critique of the consequences of implementing experiential education, both intended and unintended. These include the critique of educational management of experiential learning, the spectre of control through assessment of experiential learning that threatens encroachment into expanding spheres of adults' lives, and the potential reproduction of powerful social structures through experiential learning which suspends critical thought. These critiques lead to debates about pedagogical purpose in adults' experiential learning. Passionate opinions advocate focus on developing individuals' subjectivity, while equally fervent voices urge commitment to broader social purposes. In the following section, the contrasting arguments giving breath to these issues are outlined briefly. Resolution, if any, must occur in the practice of particular educators working in unique contexts. Further discussion of potential forms of this practice is taken up in the next chapter.

Educators' management of experiential learning has exacerbated social problems.

Important questions have been raised about any intrusion of educators into people's ongoing experiential learning. Sometimes this educational intrusion becomes management of learning for economic goals, turning experience into a productive object or knowledge—as when employees' experience is considered to be intellectual capital (Stewart, 1997) turned over to processes of knowledge management. Sometimes education is surveillance, as when adults are asked to explain their private experience to an educational group, or share it in written reflective journals and portfolios. Sometimes education views experience as a self-serving technique, something to be produced or designed, to motivate learners and enhance training. The point is that educators' consideration of and intervention in others' experiential learning are neither neutral nor innocent. Michelson (1999) claims that, in fact, educators' "management of experience has become a way of regulating how people define themselves and construct an identity" (p. 144).

For example, critical analysts of learning initiatives in workplace contexts have pointed out that, in an environment where "production is, above all, production for profit; that nature is dead, malleable matter entirely at our disposal" (Hart, 1993, p. 26), workers' experiential learning becomes human capital with great potential economic benefits for the organization. Usher and Solomon (1999) write,

> the educational discourse of experiential learning intersects happily with the managerial discourse of workplace reform . . . since both shape subjectivity in ways appropriate to the needs of the contemporary workplace. (p. 8)

In this configuration of human experience, various organizations' fight to remain competitive in a global market of overproduction, underemployment, and impossible pace of technological change (Garrick & Usher, 2000) can be transformed into a learning problem that is devolved onto individuals. Their responsibility is continuous (experiential) learning, which educators and managers assess according to knowledge claims recognized in their own particular socio-cultural milieu. As Richard Edwards (1998) argues, reflection, though differentiated, becomes a basic pedagogic stance for all workers because non-routine tasks are part of everyone's everyday work activity, not just professionals (p. 386):

> A more intense working environment may require the reflective practice of workers being able to respond on their feet . . . Here self-management within organization frameworks displaces the forms of autonomous activity which are often associated with professional work. In this sense, reflective practice may be well part of the moral technology and forms of governmentality through which work is intensified and regulated . . . Engaging in reflective practice, bringing together thought and action, reflecting whilst you are doing, are key conditions of flexibility . . . The reflective practitioner signifies the worker in reflexive modernization par excellence. (p. 387)

This shaping of the continuous (experiential) learner is perhaps the most troubling of all criticisms of the discourse of experiential learning in adult education. In the reflective/constructivist orientation, subjectivities that are potentially multiple, shifting, transgressive, and spontaneous are recast as coherent, stable, rational, and self-regulating. Their experience is raw capital to be manufactured into knowledge. The educational issue of transfer implies that fluid experience can be packaged and applied in different contexts. Experience becomes standardized, then commodified in the labor exchange relations defining capitalism.

Ironically, experiential learning's focus originated in political attempts to resist the authority of formal education and the hegemony of academic knowledge, and to honor people's own unique experiences. Models of experiential learning such as Kolb's were politically focused on liberating people from educational management by celebrating the importance of their inner experience, human dignity, and freedom to choose. However, as others have argued eloquently (Field, 2000; Finger & Asún, 2001), the impact of larger forces on educational purposes and processes is decisive. Societal trends to advance lifelong learning in service of globalized competitive "turbo-capitalism," in conditions of increasing privatization, individualization, ecological crisis, erosion of the state, and economic inequality have co-opted educators in contributing to the very social problems they hope to ameliorate.

Pedagogical assessment of experiential learning has become a tool to control lives.

Thus experiential learning and the question of legitimate pedagogical intervention cannot be discussed apart from its political, social, and cultural contexts. Assessment of prior experiential learning (APEL) is another contested practice. Critics claim that the practice of shaping and judging the worth of adults' experience through prior learning assessment processes to fit institutional standards and understandings of knowledge ensures conformity and upholds existing dominant categories of knowledge. APEL has evolved different traditions and purposes in North America and in the United Kingdom. In North America, assessment of experiential learning is typically used to help adults gain credits in postsecondary education, theoretically saving them time and money while honoring their experiential knowledge. However Michelson (1996) claims that in the process, people's experiences are subjected to the interests, authority, and understandings of knowledge pervading higher education institutions. APEL practices, she argues, distort everyday experience in the process of ripping it from the changing social contexts that give it meaning, assessing and dividing it into visible/invisible categories. People's knowing is colonized by being squeezed into APEL's preset categories and identities.

In the United Knigdom, APEL is often used for vocational accreditation. Wilma Fraser (1995) explains that the objective of programs such as Making Experience Count (MEC) was to legitimize prior learning within vocational and nonvocational certificating bodies towards awarding National Vocational Qualifications (NVQ) as well as granting standing in higher education. MEC also intended to facilitate understanding and thence ownership of the learning process, to enhance self-esteem and confidence in a process designed to be andragogical in the humanistic tradition of Malcolm Knowles. The original MEC walked a careful line between the demands for accredited outcomes to courses and a philosophy of empowering students, upholding their own life experience, and making it count.

However, Fraser argues that although originally designed to value diverse individual experience, formal and informal, APEL has restricted what counts as experience. Much potential for valuing individual experience and finding creative outlets for its expression is being eroded as market forces hold sway over issues of vocational and educational relevance. Fraser describes this as a disjuncture between public discourse and private experience, producing a fundamental paradox when the private journey of discovery and learning is brought under public scrutiny and adjudication. The underlying assumption is of a coherent unified self who excavates, narrates, and manipulates raw experience into learning. The process compels adults to construct a self to fit the APEL dimensions, and celebrates individualistic achievement: adults are what they have done. This orientation doesn't address social inequities, or the issue of different and often painful lessons learned from experiences related to our subjectivity as members of different cultural, economic, gendered environments. The so-called disadvantaged, claims Fraser, often experience great barriers to opportunity and fulfillment; it is unfair to measure them by what they have done according to institutional categories of valued and recognizable knowledge. One important area of inequity relates to the gendered nature of standards for assessing adult experience. In one example she describes how, at the School for Independent Study in London, student autobiographies were adjudicated. Fewer than 60% of women's autobiographies passed compared to 80% of men's. Fraser claims this was due to men's life patterns—as self-chosen events pursuing rational goals—being more aligned to institutional ideas. Women's life stories were parts of others' lives, with diffuse voices and shifting identities.

These critical arguments underscore the potential for pedagogy to colonize and control adults' experiential learning, ultimately creating further social problems despite its best intentions to help people. Harris (2000) suggests a complete retheorization of recognition of prior learning (RPL), scrutinizing its own power relations, contexts, and understandings of knowledge, to truly realize its potential to restore equity to credentialing practices. But Harris is insistent that RPL practices offer hope for reclaiming individuals' knowledge and life experiences in their education. Others may argue that educators and their assessments should unhitch themselves entirely from the world of everyday experience, allowing informal learning to flourish along its own direction in different communities of practice. However as the next section shows, the absence of educational intervention in forums of informal experiential learning has also resulted in problematic consequences.

Pedagogy is necessary to interrupt bad practice and the reproduction of social inequity.

Critics have pointed out that communities of practice are limited learning environments because the focus tends to be practical, social, and local, which may not suit abstract, complex learning and activities. Furthermore, not all learning in communities is laudable. Unsupervised people may make do, finding ways to participate that actually reinforce negative practices that a community is trying to eliminate. Salomon and

Perkins (1998) argue that people who are apprenticed in particular ways may pick up undesirable or incorrect forms of practice, values, or strategies that subvert or profoundly limit the collective and its participating individuals. This problematic knowledge may become fossilized through continuous reinforcement in social learning processes, and resistant to change. Communities such as workplaces also tend to conserve, protect, and recycle their knowledge, not critically challenge and extend it. Thus the natural learning processes of practice may not illuminate underlying contradictions and inequities that prevent the strengthening and growth of the community itself. Finally, natural community structures and power imbalances may exclude some learners from participation.

The situative perspective also seems silent on the issue of resistance in communities where tools and activities may be unfair or dysfunctional. Is such resistance also considered meaningful participation? And does considering all energies as participation, including those intending to disrupt and fundamentally change the system, in fact dilute their disruptive effect and ensure the continuation of the system? The situative view may be understood to assume that encouraging participation in the existing community is a good thing, and thus it provides few theoretical tools for judging what is deemed good in a particular situation or for changing a system's conventional flow of movement.

The situative perspective has yet to rigorously address the question of actors' positionality within a system. As Elizabeth Ellsworth (1997) explains, "Each time we address someone, we take up a position within knowledge, power, and desire in relation to them, and assign to them a position in relation to ourselves and to a context" (p. 54). Power flows through the system according to how these positions are connected, the way they address one another, and the nature of the resulting space between the positions. The positions are in constant flux, for they change each time someone turns to a new activity or subject. In Lave and Wenger's work (1991), a learner's positionality within a system was conceptualized simplistically as a general movement from peripheral participation to the centre of a community. This notion would be viewed as problematic from critical cultural perspectives: it presumes the existence of an identifiable centre, and appears unconcerned with the regulation of any system that accepts participation as hierarchical.

Furthermore, critics may well challenge the apolitical nature of situative views of learning. Flows of power and changing locations influence different individuals' ability to participate meaningfully in particular practices of systems. There appears not to be, among situative perspectives, satisfactory responses to certain fundamental ethical questions of learning that are posed by other perspectives, one of which is, Whose knowledge, among the various participants in the system, is afforded the greatest influence over the movements and directions of the system?

Ecological learning perspectives also don't appear to address inevitable power relations circulating in human cultural systems. Therefore the influences on patterns of coemergence exerted by culturally determined meaning categories such as gender/race/sexual orientation/ability/class/religion may be indiscernible from a systems perspective. In addition, neither systems nor situative perspectives appear to attend to the way cultural practices (such as tools of discourse, image, and representation) are determined by dominant groups in the system and how these practices continue to sustain the interests of some participants more than others. Further, a systems view of learning, such as that advanced by Peter Senge (1999) and other learning organization enthusiasts, suggests that the interests and identities of individual elements be surrendered to the greater community. Therefore, individuals potentially become vulnerable to a few who manipulate the system's discourses to sustain their own power, ensuring that their experiences become the most valued knowledge in the collective.

Pedagogy should help individuals reaffirm who they are in their experiential learning.

If people are to survive social forces threatening to fragment their lives and isolate them in ultimately meaningless pursuits to accumulate economic-valued skills, argue some, adult

education must intervene in natural learning patterns offered by
social experience. In particular, education must not avoid its important calling to help reaffirm people's subjectivity. As we saw
in Chapter 3, advocates of educational biography describe this
personal meaning-making as "the difficult process of becoming
oneself" (Dominicé, 2000, p. 80). According to this argument,
personal identity construction is adults' most crucial learning,
and it is not addressed by the situative notion of people becoming fuller participants in a community of practice. A similar
position is advanced from psychoanalytic perspectives (with
some different assumptions about how personal learning unfolds). Both challenge what appears to be the disappearance of
the subject in situative or ecological/complexity learning theories, and champion the role of pedagogy to assist individuals in
strengthening their subjectivity and working through complex
inner conflicts.

Although Davis and Sumara (1997) claim that personal
subjectivities are by no means abandoned in ecological theory
but rather understood as "mutually specifying" one another, it
is unclear how individual agency and integrity are maintained
in the "commingling of consciousness" (p. 110) that supposedly
links community and cognition seamlessly through interaction.
Those who emphasize subjectivity might wonder how, without
educational assistance, connections are made between one particular context of an individual's personal history and his or her
dynamic processes of change within other systems. Pedagogy is
argued as useful to help introduce individual knowers to theoretical knowledge existing apart from a particular community
of practice. Furthermore as shown in Chapter 3, psychoanalytic
perspectives argue that the purpose of experiential learning and
the educators facilitating it is to work through internal psychic
traumas to "craft strategies of the self."

In response to this insistence that education dwell on the
internal, situative perspectives might argue that psychoanalytic
theory pays insufficient attention to the systems that bind the
changing human mind and its psychic traumas to its changing
contexts. Jean Lave (1988) points out that context is frequently
undertheorized as some kind of container into which individu-

als are dropped. The context may be acknowledged to affect the person but the person is still viewed as an autonomous agent of knowing with his or her own fundamentally distinct psychic systems. Further, the psychoanalytic view seems to assume that learning can take place entirely as a mental process, regardless of patterns of participation in continuously evolving communities. Psychoanalytic views may mistake learning and doing, individuals and the symbolic tools and communities of their activities, as separable processes.

Kenneth Saltman (1998), from a critical cultural perspective, is concerned that so much emphasis on the personal and subjective diverts attention away from the political, the crucial power dynamics of material culture in which people need to learn to act effectively. Saltman criticizes Ellsworth, for example, for focusing on continuous re-readings of the textuality of daily life and the microstructures of the psyche. These emphases ignore the fact that microstructures are "historically contingent products of larger overdetermining social forces" (p. 10). Ultimately, says Saltman, psychoanalytic theory lays no ground for ethical or political standards in learning; for example, all versions of the Holocaust would stand. Are all workings-through to be honored and encouraged? How can we envision alternative possibilities for ourselves if all knowledge floats according to an individual's own psychic disturbances? And where, in psychoanalytic approaches to pedagogy, does the individual agency develop to change oneself and one's circumstances positively? Pushed to an extreme, this perspective may leave people in interminable ambivalence.

Pedagogy in experiential learning must be linked to purposes of social responsibility.

As we have seen, most critical cultural views urge a pedagogy imbued with a moral purpose: specifically, to bring about social transformation through experiential learning. The flowering of radical or Marxist-based adult education associated with the Brazilian educator Paulo Freire is sometimes portrayed as a historical movement with little application to contemporary contexts of globalized blurrings of identities, knowledge, nations, and capital. However, writers like Tom Heaney (1996) and Paula Allman (2001) assert emphatically that education not only can revivify this movement, it must; educators have lost their way amid relativism and ambivalence, while the need for clear purposes of social responsibility has never been greater. Finger and Asún (2001) are blunt: "adult education's main future agenda will be concerned with the linkages between learning, power and organizational change" (p. 179). Let us examine these assertions through other perspectives of learning.

Britzman's (1998a) psychoanalytic view critiques the primacy of consciousness in the critical cultural perspective, and claims that individual or collective critical reflection is a highly limited means of coming to self-knowledge. Cultural analysis may not be viewed as attending sufficiently to the forces of desire and the nuance of the unconscious in determining understandings and behaviors developed through experience. Our attempts at achieving deeper awareness by examining experience solely through rational critical thinking are thwarted by the ego's investments in maintaining its own narcissism. And ultimately, the extraordinary faith placed in human ability to achieve emancipation through self-reflexivity has been questioned. Ellsworth (1997) for example, shows how the spaces between one's critical eye and one's own ideologies—themselves both shifting and fluid—are configured by multiple desires and positional investments, and multiple contradictory readings.

Ethical issues of justice and right action become somewhat difficult to formulate in the ecological/complexity perspective. How can an educational project for change be conceived that adequately accounts for the complex ongoing systemic perturbations, without being deliberately illusory? That is, if any action of an educator or other particular element of a system becomes enfolded in that system's multiple interactions and unpredictable expansions of possibility, what sort of reference point can be used to guide intention towards some deliberate pedagogical goal? On another point, how can we explain the differential change that different elements of a system appear to register? If all interactions between people coemerge in ways that specify each other, how is it that educators often influence learners more than learners influence educators? And finally, what moral choices for wise judgment are available for educators within notions like "adequate conduct"? Because they are self-referenced (Waldrop, 1992), complex systems that many educators would abhor do often survive and expand in sustainable ways. Cancer and neo-Nazism are two examples. There must be a more defensible framework than simply coemergence to guide understandings of cognition. These questions are not reasons to reject ecological perspectives of cognition. They simply serve to point out further paradoxes that must be named as educators struggle to find ways to act within complexity.

So how is the social responsibility of pedagogy construed in traditional constructivist perspectives of experiential learning? Colin Griffin (1992) points out that Dewey was not a social radical but a pragmatist (if it works, it's true). He advocated experiential learning not particularly to empower or transform people or even to challenge existing oppressive systems of education. Rather, Dewey saw that when people worked together on projects, actively thinking about what they were doing, they took more ownership for their projects, actions, and learning, exercised more responsibility in groups, internalized concepts and mastered skills more effectively than when they were passively taught. Other educators have likewise found that incorporating experiential activity into lessons or building field-based periods into educational programs helps motivate, engage, and develop learners in significant ways. Moving away from this moderate position accepting pedagogy's role to further local social change, we confront strong resistance to the notion that pedagogy should be involved at all in social transformation.

Pedagogy should *not* presume to emancipate through experiential learning.

There has been much criticism of emancipatory views of experiential learning. Michelson (1999) observes it is now a commonplace understanding that experience, liberatory or otherwise, cannot be considered apart from "received meanings that evolve within material structures and cultural and discursive norms" (p. 141). Our identities and purposes shift according to the contexts in which we find ourselves, and the changing positions we try to enact there. We are shaped by our cultures and languages: our purposes cannot be easily separated from our investments in these communities and relationships of our everyday lives. Thus, the notion of monolithic ideologies, social structures, and large-scale causal theories is unworkable in the face of such fluid cultural expressions and practices—let alone the fantasy of emancipating people from these ideologies and structures.

Such statements reflect a particular perspective commonly associated with postmodernism—a term of much ambiguity, differentiated connotations, and diverse philosophical expressions. Writers aligning themselves with postmodern views have provided thoughtful critique of the emancipatory understanding of learning. Their questions tend to focus on the irreconcilability of fixed notions of identity, subjectivity, culture, and transformation with the complexities of plurality, motion, and ambiguity that mark human activity and meaning-making (see Lather, 1991, for an extended discussion of this point). Like Patti Lather, many of these writers work within the critical cultural tradition to refine and expand this perspective without losing its commitment to resist oppression. This is an important point for it helps illustrate how this resistance perspective, like others discussed in this article, embraces contestation and continued self-interrogation in ways that blur its own definitional boundaries. Lather's (1991) project, for example, is to theorize a defensible alignment between critical social theory and its poststructural challenges along political, social, and pedagogical grounds. Ursula Kelly (1997) incorporates Lacanian concepts within critical pedagogy to work towards a socially transformative practice informed by psychoanalytic considerations.

Ecological learning theorists do not tend to discuss power as a key dimension of systems' evolution. Nor do they emphasize the practices and discourses of human culture in explaining how communities emerge. Some reject the structural view of a dominant elite subordinating other groups as too deterministic or simplistic (rarely, outside of despotic regimes, can a group of intentional oppressors be clearly delineated). They also reject the separation of individual from the sociocultural history and dynamics of the collective. Sumara and Davis (1997) suggest that traditional frameworks of domination/oppression perpetuate negative views of power. Systems theories of learning place much greater emphasis on mutual affect, collectivity, and coemergence of human action, objects, and environment. This understanding of emerging systems supposedly transcends the negative circles created by power/resistance-based critical thinking.

Overzealous cultural critique and reconstruction are recurring pedagogical issues. Kellner (1995) cautions educators not to suppose a monolithic dominant ideology which is inherently manipulative or evil, and to remember that people are not a mass of passive, homogeneous noncritical victims of a dominant ideology. Feminist scholars have shown the repressive potential in any emancipatory efforts. Ellsworth (1992), for example, is a well-known voice among many who have questioned the possibility of creating safe pedagogical spaces where open, equitable dialogue towards empowerment can unfold. She argues that subjects are not capable of being fully rational and disinterested, that multiple meanings are endemic, and voices are contradictory and partial across and within subjects. Troubling issues about who presumes enlightenment, and how authentic democratic participation can ever be achieved through existing discourses which favor certain knowledge interests over others, have not been resolved. The irony of a democratically minded educator determining what comprises false consciousness and what conceptions of resistance should replace it, for example, has been frequently noted. Educators' positions of authority— their own intrusions and repressions, their own shaping by dominant discourses and their own will to control—are not always apparent in critical pedagogy. Then there is the problem of where learners are left after so-called empowerment. Henry Giroux (1996) shows that a new critical consciousness is not easily reconciled with the real politics of everyday life to which

most learners return; survival tactics are not typically included
in the educational agenda. When the educator is granted such
a central position in experiential learning, ethics and the limits
of educators' responsibility require address.

CONCLUSION

These issues represent only a small slice of the energetic
debates and critiques that continue among educators interested
in experiential learning. For example, a strong debate emerging
among adventure educators is that some forms of experiential
learning are becoming frivolous "edutainment du jour." Commodified for corporations and subject to market pressures, experience-based learning such as adventure activities sometimes
are stripped of important pedagogical dimensions and forced to
compromise the time required for effective planning, debrief,
and follow-through. Other important issues have been touched
upon lightly in previous chapters. For example, feminist and
antiracist educators charge that diversity in experience, particularly according to combined dimensions of gender, race/ethni-
city, sexual orientation, ableness, and class, is still widely marginalized in debates about experiential learning and appropriate
pedagogy. A related issue is learner capability and readiness (including self-concept, openness to learning, creativity, future orientation, love of learning, initiative, and willingness to accept
responsibility) for different forms of participation and learning
in experience. This invites questions not only about pedagogical
intervention but also about legitimacy of authority to judge.
Aren't capability and readiness at least partly developed through
the experience of trying something? Who presumes to determine learners' conditions of readiness or capability, according
to what criteria and for what purposes? Sharan Merriam and
Rosemary Caffarella (1999) pose many more issues for adult
educators. Some of these have been adapted and integrated with
the debates raised throughout this chapter, to construct the following list of questions for experiential educators:

- Who (learner, educator, learning community, societal need) should determine what the learning goals, directions, and opportunities should be, in different contexts?
- What are the individual's learning rights, in classroom learning, job-related learning, and community-based learning?
- To what extent can public good be reconciled with learner freedom?
- To what extent should experiential education focus upon social responsibility and to what extent upon learner's subjectivity, in different contexts?
- At what point and in what situations is pedagogical interference in processes of individual and social change through experiential learning unwarranted or at worst, unethical?
- At what point does pedagogical intervention in experiential learning become management for social control?
- In different circumstances of pedagogical intervention, how should educators define the reach of their responsibilities — for extent of long-term learning, for learners' traumas and joys, and for design elements such as learning environment and activity?
- What role, if any, has assessment in different contexts of experiential learning? How can assessment be conducted without doing violence to people's experiences?

This chapter has described the theoretical and pedagogical issues that lie at the heart of these questions and has shown different perspectives on these issues contributed by constructivist, psychoanalytic, situative, critical cultural, and ecological learning theories. At bottom, these issues tend to center on understanding the relations between individual, situation, society, and environment in experiential learning, the nature of mind in action, and the ethical role of the educator. In particular, we have seen concerns raised about the increasing tensions between individual and society confronted in different ways by different perspectives. Finger and Asún (2001) describe ominous trends in what they describe as a growing societal focus on individualistic experiential learning: loss of collective and individual meaning, lack of responsibility for societal and cultural erosion, and the increasing privatization and commercialization of adult education to promote capitalism. Vandenabeele and Wildemeersch (2000) from a social learning perspective write that the entire interaction between individual/society (configurations) is about identity: "critical reflection is not only a rational activity, but also an activity strongly related to continuous processes of identity construction, embedded in processes of interaction and communication" (p. 127).

Clearly no one pedagogical approach responds adequately to these deeper concerns. However, educators can explore and combine different roles and methodological approaches in their own practice. The next chapter presents a range of positions and actions that educators have adopted, borrowing from suggestions offered by the different models of experiential learning in this book. While traditional roles such as facilitating dialogue and coaching skills are represented, educators can also play important roles by adjusting a physical environment, offering questions, suggesting projects, bringing together people with different views, pointing out the uncanny, or introducing an unexpected resource.

CHAPTER 5

So What? Roles for Adult Educators

Clandinin and Connelly (1995) write, "The sources for evidence for understanding knowledge, and the places knowledge may be said to reside exist not only in the mind but in the narratives of personal experience. With Dewey (1938), we see thinking not so much as an act of mind but as temporal, narrative expressions located in mind, in storied reconstructions of experience, and in practice" (p. 269). How can we as teachers bring to the fore learners' various selves—rational, gendered, intellectual, interior, exterior—to enable the personalization of their learning through meaningful experience? How can we as learners develop the skills to incorporate the strengths of our own life experiences into the shape of our learning and teaching?

Given what appear to be conflicting orientations to experiential learning and the various critiques each presents about the different educational practices that have proliferated around experiential learning, practitioners might be justified in feeling some frustration about how to proceed. The question remains, What has all of this to say to the practice of adult education? This chapter begins to address this question by focusing on suggested roles for adult educators working with experiential learning. These vary widely according to different perspectives of experiential learning, from recommendations for planning and evaluating learners' experience to views of the educator as embedded in the experience itself. The purpose here is to present a wide array of pedagogical postures and entry points for occasions of experiential learning from which educators may choose, rather than emphasize the distinctions between theoretical understandings of educational roles. Table 5.1 summarizes some roles associated with the five perspectives of constructivism, situative theory, psychoanalytic theory, critical cultural perspectives, and complexity theory.

So, how are we to make sense of these different roles? There is no one role for any one educator, for an adult educator's vocation encompasses a variety of demands and tasks requiring different postures. Depending on the purposes, desires, and capabilities of all participants (including the educator), some educational situations emphasize active design and facilitation by educators. Others benefit from the educator's silence and patient waiting. Some require assessment and others require none at all. Meanwhile, each of us feels more comfortable and philosophically aligned with certain educational roles over others. The following list may serve to remind us of the myriad ways of entering experience with other adults towards enhancing learning—our own as well as theirs.

ROLES FOR FOSTERING REFLECTION
UPON EXPERIENCE
(Constructivist Perspective)

In the constructivist view of experiential learning, where individuals are presumed to actively interpret their worlds and create their own knowledge through reflective processes, adult educators have suggested various roles for themselves to enhance learners' reflection. In this section, four are discussed. First is the role of facilitator, where adult educators encourage people to recall, value, talk about, and perhaps critically analyse their own past experience to construct knowledge from it. Second is the role of catalyst, where educators create a happening during instruction designed to engage learners experientially and thus encourage construction of knowledge. Third is the role of coach, where an educator guides learners to reflect on choices in the "hot action" of experience, so they will analyse undesirable outcomes and make corrections. Fourth is the role of asses-

Table 5.1 Purposes, Roles, and Activities for Educators in Different Theoretical Orientations to Experiential Learning

Perspective	Educator's Purposes	Educator's Roles	Activities, Designs, and Occasions for Learning
Reflecting upon concrete experience **Constructivist theory**	• Encourage reflective process. • Pose challenges to individual assumptions. • Validate knowledge acquired through personal construction.	• Facilitating reflection. Instigating concrete experience. • Coaching. • Assessing experiential learning.	• Adventure learning. • Environmental education. • Problem-based learning. • Project learning and classroom laboratory. • Coaching strategies. • Mentoring. • Reflecting critically on work experience.
Participating in a community of practice **Situative theory**	• Arrange conditions in complex social situations that help learners best practice the kinds of participation they desire. • Intervene through coaching or cognitive apprenticeship.	• Studying effective participation. • Designing environments. • Enabling opportunities. • Coaching participation.	• Service learning. • Designing situative learning environments. • Cognitive apprenticeship. • Facilitating action learning. • Direct and indirect guidance.
Attuning to unconscious desires and fears **Psychoanalytic theory**	• Accept own psychic dilemmas of love/hate. • Facilitate learners' psychic self-analysis. • Honor the difficulty, time, and limits of learning as working through psychic conflicts. • Avoid rescue fantasies.	• Studying desire and identity. • Promoting interference of daily encounters, thoughts. • Drawing attention to psychic dilemmas. • Teaching deep analysis. • Clearing spaces for difficult knowledge. • Attending with compassion.	• Encouraging reflective autobiography. • Multiple text readings. • Confronting difficult knowledge. • Decoding workplace language and environment. • Understanding one's desires and anxieties in work.
Resisting dominant social norms of experience **Critical cultural theories**	• Help make explicit the ideologies, practices, and positioning that construct experience in particular ways. • Open spaces for and support resistance. • Help seek beyond current struggles to craft social alternatives.	• Studying power. • Posing problems. • Facilitating dialogue. • Challenging beliefs, norms. • Gathering the collective. • Motivating resistance. • Empowering leaders. • Supporting transformation.	• Facilitating problem-posing. • Popular education. • Emancipatory learning through social action.
Exploring ecological relationships between cognition and environment **Complexity theories**	• Track patterns and relations in complex adaptive systems. • Assist participants to understand and connect with the system. • Promote change in dysfunctional patterns. • Support healing patterns. • Be clear about one's own entanglement in the emerging systems of thought and action.	• Studying complex systems. • Being an interpreter by connecting parts to whole, facilitating participants' naming/renaming of changing nuances outside and inside. • Being a noisemaker by creating disequilibrium, amplifying disturbances. • Being a mapmaker by providing feedback to system, tracking systemic changes. • Influencing discourses, stories.	• Opening spaces for community dialogue: Open Space, Future Search. • Disequilibrium, amplification, and feedback. • Occasioning. • Organic structures.

sor, where educators represent, judge, and give credit to people's experiences in terms of the kind of knowledge they have constructed from these experiences. Obviously these roles are not distinct and separate in practice, but are often blended.

Caffarella, Barnett, and Bruce (1994) created a model for educators working with experiential learning, based on constructivism, that brings together four basic considerations: learner differences, Kolb's model of concrete experience alternating with reflection, engaging activities, and assessment that honors experience.

1. *Characteristics and needs of learners.* Attending to learners' prior knowledge and experience, their different processes, the contexts of their lives, and their affiliation (belonging) needs.

2. *Conceptual foundations of experiential learning.* Constructivist understandings of learning, especially Kolb's theory of concrete experience, then reflection on that experience and Schön's theory of reflective practice.

3. Methods and techniques for engaging learners in experiential learning activities. Designing in-class activities, designing field experiences, and creating situations where learners' past experiences are discussed and processed.

4. *Assessment processes and outcomes.* Portfolios and other self-assessment practices that honor individual experiences and personal knowledge constructed from them.

This model assumes that an educative event involves a classroom, an educator designing programs and evaluating people's progress, activities specifically focused on learning, and an assumption that people learn by reflecting on experience. This assumption is common among the following four roles based on constructivist understandings of learning—facilitator, catalyst, coach, and assessor—but is not shared by advocates of certain other perspectives, whose suggestions for the educator's role are described later in this chapter.

Facilitator of Reflection

When Malcolm Knowles (1970) focused attention on the importance of adults' experience in their learning and the pedagogical value of reflecting on that experience, adult educators began to view themselves as facilitators of learning. Their role shifted from dispensing information and concepts to encouraging people to thoughtfully analyse their experiences. Educational suggestions grounded in Knowles's concepts included directives such as the following:

- Learners' past experience should be honored, given voice, shared, and compared.
- Learners should be assisted to link specific past experience with their current situations.
- Learners' past experience should be analyzed in terms of their beliefs (about themselves, how things work, what is important, and what things mean).

It is evident in the very way that constructivist theories are presented in the preceding section that adults processing their everyday experiences are often viewed as learners needing a facilitator's help to construct the best possible knowledge from these experiences. David Boud and his associates (1996), for example, suggest that people may need help to develop the special skills and strategies for noticing, intervening, and later reevaluating their experience with sufficient depth to construct worthwhile new knowledge from it. Experiential learning involves strong emotions, explain Boud and his associates. It requires an environment of trust, authenticity, integrity, and mutual respect—as well as patience with each other on the part of all participants: learners as well as facilitator. Denis Postle (1993) explains his practice working with learners' emotions, grounded in John Heron's (1992) multimodal learning theory.[1] Postle developed criteria to assess the emotional competence that influences people's learning in the fourth affective mode (such as understanding and being able to express feelings freely, transmute and release feelings, and self-monitor emotions. The idea is that facilitators can help people identify and even self-assess their emotional involvement in personal experience, to expand and enrich their learning.

For many people personal self-disclosure is uncomfortable in group settings. They would prefer solitude and self-dialogue to critical reflection in conversation. And as Boud's team (1996) also concluded, there may be periods in our lives when we are more predisposed to reflection on experiential learning. There may be a readiness factor at work, a reflective learning style, or a life-span issue of particular crises or transitions that prompt our motivation to reflect critically on who we are and where we're going. Some theorists have questioned the assumption that every adult is capable of or even interested in critical reflection.

Dorothy MacKeracher (1996) advises facilitators wishing to promote reflection and critical reflection on experience to create conditions for open, honest dialogue by spending time building community among learners. Facilitators need to be bold, encouraging probes of sensitive or possibly conflictive topics, and raising difficult questions that are easy to sidestep. Facilitators are helpful in pointing out assumptions that are embedded in a group discussion, or noting issues that are being omitted or ignored. They name emotions and contradictions that lurk under the surface of a discussion, pointing out the dynamics of politics and positioning going on constantly without enraging dialogue participants. Good facilitators are also skillful in balancing the voices of a discussion, ensuring that there is space made for everyone. However, feminist educators such as Elizabeth Tisdell (1995) remind facilitators to continually attend to power relations inherent in any group—particularly one structured by the authoritative presence of a teacher—to identify all stakeholders and their participation in the dialogue, to consider the levels of inclusivity, and to be conscious of ways unconscious behavior contributes to reproducing unequal power relations.

Stephen Brookfield (1993) exhorts educators to revisit and analyse their own visceral experiences before asking learners to do so. In fact, Brookfield encourages educators to emulate his own practice of narrating a personal experience publicly to a group of learners, and inviting them to critically analyse it for assumptions informing his choices or framing his view of the situation. Afterwards, he invites learners in small groups to do the same, narrating their own experience and subjecting it to the respectful critical insights of their colleagues.

Facilitator of Transformation

Mezirow's (1991, 2000) theory of transformative learning has inspired a wide range of educational activities designed to help adults break outside of their own natural and perhaps limited or even distorted ways of viewing their own experience, and reflect more critically. These activities help people achieve transformation by prompting deep reflection leading to desirable refinement or dramatic change in their meaning perspectives. In synthesizing the findings of several studies outlining ideal educative conditions for fostering transformative learning, Edward Taylor (1998) offers the following list of suggestions for educators:

• Promote a sense of safety, openness, and trust.
• Support a learner-centered approach, student autonomy, participation, and collaboration.
• Encourage exploration of alternative personal perspectives, problem-posing, and critical reflection.
• Be trusting, emphatic, caring, and authentic, and demonstrate a high degree of integrity.
• Emphasize personal self-disclosure.
• Discuss and work through emotions before critical reflection.
• Provide feedback and encourage self-assessment.

David Deshler (1990) is one of many who suggest that facilitators encourage learners to reflect on the language they use to represent their own experience. Our language is packed with metaphors which construct our attitudes and assumptions to our experiences in particular ways. Consider the use of military metaphors in the workplace such as strategic position, targets, attacking problems, the front lines, and lose the battle to win the war. Deshler suggests that facilitators help people surface the metaphors shaping their experiences, critically examine them through dialogue with others, then reconstruct those metaphors that limit, distort, or repress significant dimensions of experience.

Elizabeth Saavedra (1996) worked with teachers over two years to identify conditions that promote transformative learning in a group setting. Her list synthesizes many of the foregoing ideas:

1. *Dialogic context.* The group meets in a safe space where all voices are honored in democratic, collaborative dialogue.

2. *Identity and voice.* Participants each are encouraged to explore their own identities and identity construction through race, gender, and class experiences.

3. *Ownership and agency.* Group participants actively negotiate the intent of the group.

4. *Dissonance and conflict.* Conflict is embraced and worked through collaboratively.

5. *Mediational events and demonstrations.* Group participants lead authentic learning events, and different interpretations of discussion topics are mediated.

6. *Reflection, action, and generation.* Participants are encouraged to reflect on the group process, and act to enhance it.

7. *Self-assessment and evaluation.* Group members have space to critically reflect in the company of others on their own practice.

8. *Reflective practice.* Personal stock-taking, applying the critical reflection approaches developed in the group, becomes a daily practice.

These eight conditions clearly depend on intentional facilitation. The educator's role implied here is to initiate and sustain democratic dialogue, modeling and perhaps teaching participants how to listen with respect, contribute with confidence, confront dissonance, and actively ensure inclusivity. The educator must be a careful critical observer and skillful questioner, probing participants to notice and analyse issues that emerge in the dialogue, in the encounters, and in personal matters related to identity and intent. But the educator also must be able to relinquish control by involving participants, then having them lead group negotiations of objectives, meaning, learning, and self-assessment.

The purposes of Saavedra, Deshler, Mezirow, Brookfield, MacKeracher, and Boud are similar: to establish, as Taylor (1998) puts it, "a learning situation that is democratic, open, rational, has access to all available information, and promotes critical reflection." Overall, however, a common conclusion is that educators need not so much to use particular techniques as to be committed to transformative learning themselves. Patricia Cranton has written extensively about facilitating transformative learning, and suggests that above all educators should be "adult learners continually striving to update, develop, expand, and deepen their professional perspectives both on their subject areas and on their goals and roles" (1996, p. 228). This means becoming critically reflective ourselves about our philosophies, our assumptions about learners, and our practices. This also means being willing to learn and change ourselves in the process of helping others to learn—which sometimes means facing painful truths.

Catalyst of Active Learning Experiences

As discussed earlier, experiential learning can result from eliciting adults' past experience and encouraging focused reflection and analysis of it, from coaching someone to reflect during actual situated experience, or from creating an experiential happening. Usually the latter approach is related to formal education, an institutional classroom or training session where an educator wishes to engage the learners physically and emotionally. Such created experiences are considered most effective when reflection for learning is carefully layered into the experience, usually through dialogue debriefing the experience.

Adult educators have experimented with a variety of creative ways to involve learners physically, emotionally, and relationally as well as cognitively in learning activities. Simulations are one example. For example, each person is given a particular role with its own agenda, history, and resources, and then assigned a task requiring interaction with others to achieve his or her goal. Instructional games and ice breakers are also widely available (i.e., Newstrom & Scannell, 1980; Renner, 1994). Role-play is often used to practice interpersonal skills (for example, having pairs act out situations to explore possible approaches to handling them). Another way is to improvise a scenario to see what might happen if particular actions are taken. Popular theatre technique has been adapted to adult education as an instrument of personal empowerment and cultural intervention (Prentki & Selman, 2000). Physical problem-solving games and activities have been borrowed from adventure education for use in formal classroom learning. The point is to stimulate participants' creativity by compelling them to act in unfamiliar situations. Problem-based learning or PBL is becoming increasingly common in professional education (Colliver, 2000). Educators design a dilemma based in "real" contexts of practice, act as resources while learners work through the dilemma to create a response or solution, then help learners reflect critically on the process to articulate conclusions and apply the information and skills developed. Further details and examples of these activities are provided in Chapter 6.

Longer-term (such as two- or three-day workshops) adventure-based education activities have become a popular form of experiential learning to build teams, develop leadership or creativity, and enhance problem-solving and conflict management skills. Educators design, lead and debrief such activities to maximize learners' benefit (Gass & Gillis, 1995). Project-based learning is also longer term, where an educator helps learners design and conduct an individual or group project rooted in real community or workplace situations. While learners self-direct much of the activity, the educator assumes important roles as guide, design consultant, outfitter and resource assistant, trouble-shooter, and experience analyst. Internship and apprenticeship terms offer work-based experiential learning opportunities, typi-cally initiated, coordinated, and facilitated by an educator. Serv-ice learning is similar, but involves learners in community-based service projects such as removing graffiti, working in neighbor-hood soup kitchens, or mentoring elementary children (Howard, 1993). Educators not only catalyse the community partnership and project development, but also help learners integrate formal learning of skills and knowledge with the service experience.

Writers advocating the use of any of these experiential learning approaches seem to agree that the educator's role as catalyst includes ensuring three dimensions: preparation, envi-ronment, and reflection. First, learners must be *prepared* appro-priately. Many adults fear or dislike such activities because they have suffered humiliation being forced to participate in over-whelmingly unfamiliar experiences without competence. Role-play exercises, for example, require preparation for focus, imagi-native spontaneity, trust, and physical and verbal fluency. Drama instructors use extensive warm-up activities before engaging learners in role-plays. Educators might consult a resource such as Viola Spolin's (1963) book *Improvisation for the Theatre* for suggested approaches. Preparation also means alerting learners to the purpose of an activity. The second dimension is *environ-ment*, referring to the need for a respectful community where participants are safe from being laughed at or hurt. Respectful communities do not simply happen. Good facilitators build them through clear expectations, continual reminders, and even direct instruction about supporting one another. Activities should also allow an opt-out choice for learners who feel un-comfortable participating. The third dimension of *reflection* re-quires time after the experience for absorbing one's responses to what happened, talking with others to compare meanings, identifying desirable and undesirable consequences, and form-ing questions and conclusions for future.

Coach of Experiential Learning

An abundant body of literature has accumulated around the twin notions of coaching and mentoring in adult education. Unlike the role of facilitator of experiential learning, mentors and coaches usually work one-on-one with someone *in situ*, that is, within the actual context of a person's practice. For Laurent Daloz (1999), mentors play a significant role in an adult's development and transformation by providing support, structure, positive expectations, self-disclosure, challenging tasks and questions, advocacy, high standards, modeling, maps, language, and a mirror for an adult's growth. Daloz describes mentors as "guides":

> They lead us along the journey of our lives. We trust them because they have been there before. They embody our hopes, cast light on the way ahead, interpret arcane signs, warn us of lurking dangers, and point out unexpected delights along the way. There is a certain luminosity about them, and they often pose as magicians in tales of transformation. (p. 18)

By contrast, coaching is usually associated with specific skill learning. For example, professional practitioners such as teachers, doctors, nurses, accountants, and lawyers experience a period of internship as part of their training, where they are assigned to a particular organization to carry out regular duties with the assistance of a coach—an experienced practitioner familiar with the organizational context. One model of the coach's role in this activity is known as clinical supervision. In this model the coach commits to several periods of focused observation, watching the practitioner carrying out everyday work tasks. The observational period ideally is preceded by a preobservation conference, a dialogue in which the practitioner clarifies the purposes and the proposed methods for the tasks, and the coach offers suggestions and states the focuses for observation. The observational period is followed by a postobservation conference of reflective dialogue. Here the coach and the practitioner together review what happened by comparing meanings, identify and analyse any dilemmas of practice that emerged, examine the practitioner's choices and rationale, generate alternative choices, and plan future sessions. The cycle is repeated several times. The point is that while the supervisor may offer suggestions, the emphasis is more on encouraging the practitioner to reflect on the experience towards improvement. Extensive literature on clinical supervision suggests that the coach adapt coaching style to the developmental stage and particular developmental needs of practitioners (Siens & Ebmeier, 1996), as well as providing feedback that will accomplish the following:

- Help practitioners learn the language of their practice, so they can name what they see happening.
- Encourage practitioners to note patterns they want to change, and establish goals for their own improvement.
- Offer questions to encourage practitioners' specific reflection, such as: (1) How do you decide what you are going to do? (2) What methods do you typically use? (3) How do you know if you have been successful? (4) What changes have you made to your methods?

Assessor of Experiential Learning

Prior learning assessment (PLA) is a process being adopted by many postsecondary institutions and adult education programs through which learners seek academic course credit for their life experiences. Many adults have developed valuable knowledge and skills throughout their study, work, travel, volunteer, family, and leadership experiences in life outside a formal education program. PLA tries to recognize this life experience so that learners can avoid repeating courses presenting knowledge they have already gained, and show they have met the entry requirements to enter courses at their own level of understanding and skill. Most PLA processes use a variety of tools designed to help learners reflect on, articulate, and demonstrate their past learning. Here are some examples of common tools:

- *Portfolio*. Learners assemble a file containing descriptions of their learning supported with documentation: samples of their work, letters from supervisors, demonstrations of accomplishments, and so on.

- *Analysis*. Learners critically assess their life and work experiences and describe the specific learning outcomes they have developed through these experiences.
- *Skill development profile*. Learners complete a variety of questionnaires self-assessing their prior experiential learning and their areas for future skill development.
- *Challenge tests*. Learners challenge a particular course by completing various written and nonwritten assessment activities, including tests, simulations, interviews, and so on.
- *Interview*. Learners are interviewed to help them articulate their achievements and the learning outcomes of their past experience.

The institution then matches the learner's experiential learning as reflected in PLA to its own established academic standards, so that credit can be awarded by a credentialing body. Many learners need help completing a PLA, and institutions often provide workshops to assist them. PLA provides a rare opportunity to explore life experiences and accomplishments in depth; it can really build learner's confidence and pride. PLA also can be a helpful ongoing process of reflection and self-assessment for the learner. It focuses on competency and understandings rather than grades, and is often billed as a useful career planner. It helps learners actually recognize what they know and can do.

The downside of PLA, as Michelson (1996) points out, is the difficulty of articulating experiential learning. Not all learners have the means to express or demonstrate their understandings, especially when PLA often depends on writing ability. Second, institutions ask learners to organize their life experiences according to only those competencies and concepts that the institution has decided are valuable. This may narrow and exclude the rich experiences of many adult learners. As Judy Harris (1999) concurs, processes commonly used for recognition of prior learning can be prescriptive and limiting. They can be easily dominated by the excessive power of institutions to determine where the knowledge boundaries are placed, and how the learner's experience is to be regulated to fit particular hierarchical categories of experience that are deemed worthy of recognition. Harris also suggests that there are different, more inclusive ways to assess adults' prior learning. She suggests that knowledge boundaries be negotiated among learners, academics, and representatives of workplace or other contexts in which learners must function. These negotiations may encourage a permeability of boundaries and recognize contextualized, action-oriented knowledge produced in social practices, as well as knowledge that fits disciplinary categories.

In reality, these four educator roles in experiential learning—facilitator, catalyst, coach, and assessor—often blur within the actual activities that unfold in a learning event. Throughout the four roles and suggestions for educators discussed in the previous section, four themes are apparent. One is engaging learners in concrete experience as a starting point for building new knowledge. Second is creating conditions for educative dialogue during and after the concrete experience. Third is encouraging learners' focused reflection at different levels, and fourth is providing support, as experiential learning can be confusing, emotionally challenging, unfamiliar, and uncomfortable for learners.

ROLES FOR ENHANCING PARTICIPATION IN A COMMUNITY OF PRACTICE
(Situative Perspective)

From the situative perspective the educator's role is not to develop individuals, but to help them participate meaningfully in the practices they choose to enter. James Greeno (1997) characterizes this pedagogical goal as improved participation in an activity. People "improve" by becoming more attuned to constraints and affordances of different real situations. The educator may arrange authentic conditions and activities in which the learners practice interacting. When people learn to notice how specific properties and relations influence their possibilities for acting in one situation, they can more easily transform that activity in a wider range of situations (Greeno, 1997). However Greeno's portrayal of the helping educator contradicts certain premises of situated cognition, for the deliberate insertion of an actor with particular intentions changes the purpose and flow of the activity. Educators cannot regard their own participation separately from the overall negotiation of the question, What constitutes meaningful participation in this community? In this respect, aspects of role-taking as coach and facilitator described in preceding sections are useful for enhancing people's participation. In addition, situative literature suggests educator roles as environmental designers, just-in-time coaches, story shifters, and mediators for action learning.

Environmental Designer

Much research has explored the possibilities of designing environments that promote embodied, situative learning. In classroom practice the objective is to simulate "authentic" activities and situations of practice containing rich, multifaceted problems that learners must identify and work through (Cognition and Technology Group at Vanderbilt, 1990). Research on effective ways to assist situative learning in the workplace has also emphasized ways to arrange environmental and cultural conditions to optimize learning, such as Stephen Billett's (2001) work on direct and indirect guidance (see Chapter 6). Others claim the pedagogical value of the situated perspective is to illuminate how different elements of a learning environment interact to produce particular actions and goals. Following this, Brent Wilson and Karen Myers (1999) propose these questions for educators: "Is the learning environment successful in accomplishing its learning goals? How do the various participants, tools and objects interact together? What meanings are constructed? How do the interactions and meanings help or hinder desired learning?" (p. 242). Anna Sfard (1998) points out that when educators emphasize the participation metaphor, themes of togetherness, solidarity, and collaboration are invoked which can promote more positive risk-taking and inquiry in learning environments. Further, educators can continue reminding participants in a learning situation over time that they are in constant flux, which avoids any permanent labeling of people:

> . . . for the learner, all options are always open, even if he or she carries a history of failure. Thus quite unlike the [acquisition of knowledge] metaphor, the [participation metaphor] seems to bring a message of an everlasting hope: Today you act one way; tomorrow you may act differently. (Sfard, 1998, p. 8)

Coaching "Anticipative Action"

David Beckett (2001) explains the learning that occurs continually in the hot action of workplace practice as "anticipative action." When conditions are changing so rapidly that the exact skills required to achieve a particular objective are not always mastered, as in today's workplaces, people still attempt to press on. They draw as much as possible from a repertoire of previously learned patterns and rules of operating, but blend this mastery with improvisation. This improvisation is a process of moving on beyond the known patterns, trying and risking, with intention but not certainty: what Beckett calls confident extrapolation. In this extrapolation we cannot plan absolutely for the contingent, but we create possibilities and mentally rehearse our accomplishments almost simultaneously as we observe and adjust the effects of our actions in the moment. Thus, we "feedforward," a process that Beckett distinguishes from the popular notion of "feedback" which, he explains, merely provides information about past experiments that may not have further application. Feedforwarding is a reflexive process of anticipating our actions, negotiating and renegotiating them in actual changing conditions.

The educator's role, Beckett argues, is in providing just-in-time assistance to enable confident action in situations where confident competence is lacking. In Beckett's examples this assistance is often web-based with some help from roving human facilitators. However extrapolating from Beckett's ideas, I would suggest that the educator also may play a useful role in assisting those who are unable for whatever reason to keep moving ahead. When people freeze in situations where they feel they lack competence, educators might coach them in skills of antici-pative action: trying small-scale experiments, trusting one's in-stincts, creating on the spot, drawing on all available resources, putting failure into perspective, and not obsessing about errors.

Story-Shifter

Jeff Gold and his colleagues (2000) show that for a com-munity of practice to shift by adopting a new practice or vision, its storytelling must change. For example, an organization com-mitted to responding to particular community issues such as housing needs, antiglobalization, environmental restoration and the like, has stories that knit together its values and history, its sense of enemies and friends, that are kept alive through every-day talk. Educators can intentionally catalyse innovative prac-tice or a change in the organization's thinking about itself, but the process is a long-term shift among these stories. Gold and his colleagues argue that for any learning intervention to be re-ceived as valid and acceptable in a community of practice— whether a new vision or the adoption of a technology designed to help the community solve particular problems—the innova-tion must first be aligned with the fundamental values and sto-ries of that community. Then the change in practice can be in-troduced into the community's ongoing learning networks -its talk, memos, and documents—by facilitators. Educators can shift old stories to the new discourse through repetition, pro-moting new terms and embedding the new talk in new stories that resonate powerfully with the community's deepest values. When the change eventually becomes part of the community's story-telling it becomes imbued with a sufficient reality to gain legitimacy as community knowledge, and becomes enmeshed with community members' own interests.

Action Learning Mediator

One popular form of pedagogical intervention inspired by the situative perspective is action learning or action-reflection learning. This form of experiential learning, particularly prevalent in workplace organizations, combines authentic group problem solving with critical reflection (Revans, 1980). Educators assist the process with a variety of approaches in roles as catalyst and facilitator, described in further detail in Chapter 6. In addition, educators can make useful contributions as mediators of the overall process. In this role, educators promote action learning to managers, track the issues that emerge, adjust the program accordingly, and compile evidence of the various results of the experiential learning process over time. In one example described by Jennifer Bowerman and John Peters (1999), educators assessed an action learning initiative for leadership development that they facilitated in a large bureaucratic organization. As Bowerman and Peters show, many important benefits of experiential learning are not necessarily visible, testable, or completely developed at the time the organization wants evidence of outcomes. These outcomes included learners' gradually increasing maturity, appreciation for each other's perspectives, emerging critical and self-directed learning abilities, as well as projects in varying stages of development and success throughout the organization.

An important role is played by the educator in tracking the process and collecting multiple evidences of positive changes (ranging from learners' self-evaluations to project descriptions and artifacts demonstrating degrees of positive change related to the project implementations). The educator also may need to mediate between some managers' expectation of quantifiable evidence, and the nature of ongoing, qualitative changes related to experiential learning. Bowerman and Peters also refer to the importance of documenting and reporting experiential learning programs, citing their own growth through the process of attempting to capture, frame, and explain the complexity of the different events the emerged throughout the initiative. Finally, an important conclusion offered by Bowerman and Peters is the need for some readiness on the part of the participants, the managers, and the organizational structure itself in an experiential learning effort. Participants require some maturity and willingness to take responsibility to learn their own way through a project; managers must be sufficiently patient for the slow, nonlinear process required by people experimenting with new behaviors; and the organization must be ready to truly allow critical thinking, mistakes, and time for people to work through new learning.

ROLES FOR ATTUNING TO UNCONSCIOUS DESIRES AND FEARS
(Psychoanalytic Perspective)

The role of the educator is a problem from the psychoanalytic view because its impulse is to solve the problem of learners' conflicts. But these conflicts are not knowledge deficits or insufficiently developed meaning perspectives to be liberated through conscious critical reflection or an educator's intervention, claim psychoanalysts. Britzman (1998a) for example deplores education's urgent compulsion to emancipate and produce learners' change. She argues that such pedagogy often represses psychic conflict in its intolerance of complex individual learning processes of working-through. Education instead, Britzman claims, should help people come to know and value the self's dilemmas as elegant problems and allow space and time for workings-through. The conditions and dynamics for the slow, difficult, and interminable work of learning itself are what should be at stake, not content or particular versions of cognitive change.

Meanwhile, educators need to accept the reality that their underlying dream of absolute completion of knowledge in learners is impossible, for the unconscious escapes intentionality and meaning, and is often completely unrecognized by both the learner and the educator (Felman, 1987). That is, whatever lessons are available in a particular experience for learning through participation and reflection, the unconscious will interfere with its own purposes and resistances. Further, one cannot set out to directly educate the unconscious—say, by changing those deep desires or fears getting in the way of one learning all that an experience has to offer—because these drives are not rational or trainable. In fact, Felman points out that the powerful dynamic among the learner, other actors, and the educator is formed between the relations of one unconscious to another, and is unknowable to all participants. To learn, people need not to overcome their inner conflicts and unconscious struggles with the nuances of the experiences, but to try to understand, accept, and redirect these learning conflicts—celebrating the self that is emerging from them. Educators can help others to do so, but only after they have themselves delved deeply into their own personal "traumas of the self." Two roles suggested by the psychoanalytic perspective are educator as interferer and educator as analyst-listener.

Interferer

As we saw in Chapter 2, Deborah Britzman (1998a) views learning psychoanalytically as interference of conscious thought by the unconscious, and the uncanny psychic conflicts that result. Learning happens by working through the conflicts of all these psychic events, in a process Britzman calls "everyday strategies of crafting the self." Experiential learning is thus coming to tolerate our own conflicting desires, while accepting and attempting to understand those disturbing or irrational parts of our selves that we work so hard to repress. When we understand these, we can find more productive ways to cope with our deepest desires and fears.

The educator's role is to promote this interference—bothering the conscious mind, and interrupting learners' sense of truth. For example, educators can alert learners to the indications of inner conflict, and encourage learners to monitor and work through these for themselves: dreams and daydreams, odd slips of speech, sudden unexplained thoughts or images, repeated behavioral patterns defying conscious choices, evidence of obsessions, odd coincidences, avoidance of things that would promote one's conscious objectives, and so on. Educators can invite learners to attend more carefully to these uncanny experiences, and analyse them in terms of tracing one's deeper desires and fears, loves and hates. Learners can be encouraged to accept whatever these psychic incidents reveal about oneself, then seek strategies to meet these inner needs in acceptable ways.

As facilitators, educators also can interfere with learners' immediate ways of responding to and interpreting experience, by helping learners probe their own reactions, behaviors, and attributions—always seeking evidence of the unconscious at work. As catalysts, educators can highlight inner conflict by engaging learners in contrasting texts, such as pictures, films, and stories, or texts representing similar experiences in contradictory ways. Or, educators might present people with texts contradicting the learners' own experience and interpretations of it. The ensuing analyses, perhaps in dialogue or in learners' personal writing, focus on the learner responses emerging from this interference with their consciously constructed meanings, looking carefully for traces of the unconscious.

An obvious issue that educators need to attend to with such approaches is the prohibition to such dialogue sustained through power relationships and authority structures operating in a group or classroom. Invasion of private spaces, associations of the confessional, presumptions to control through knowing subjects, issues of transference, and multiple inequities make the classroom a charged political space where psychoanalytic workings-through must be broached with exceeding caution.

Analyst-Listener

As Deborah Britzman (1998a) emphasizes, the teacher is most definitely not a psychoanalyst, nor is the classroom the environment for psychoanalysis. However, educators must listen to their experiences to discern traces of their own unconscious desires—desires for certainty, for students' love, for authority—in their actions and responses to events. Britzman urges us to examine those sites of our own resistance to knowing, the dark shadows of our fears and guilt within our practice interacting with learners. By examining our own educational biographies, we can seek revealing contradictions, ambiguities, and love-hate conflicts in our learning and practice. When we as educators come to know our own self conflicts and how these are manifest in our pedagogy, we learn to tolerate difficult knowledge and the difficult workings-through that students experience in coming to confront their own conflicts. In other words, to be effective helping students work through their psychic dilemmas, we need to learn to listen to our own unconscious.

Moving away from introspection to classroom practice, Elizabeth Ellsworth (1997) suggests that how the teacher speaks and listens is more important than what the teacher says. Teaching can be understood as the unconscious of teacher and student in a reciprocal relationship—both push away what they don't want to know, yet both are drawn to one another. She characterizes the unconscious as the third participant in any teacher-student relationship, which continually unsettles the communication and unfolding of knowledge:

> All learning and knowing takes a detour through the discourse of the Other—through the unconscious and opaque dynamics of social and cultural prohibition. And it is because of the presence of this third term that speaks not directly, but through substitutions, displacements, dreams and slips of the tongue, that learning cannot proceed directly. (p. 64)

Her suggestion is for educators to respect and listen carefully to this third participant of the unconscious, which emerges in responses to texts and events of both learners and educators. Her book offers examples of the uncanny emotions, resistance to texts, and puzzling moments of incomprehension in teaching that can open spaces for the unconscious. Such listening is difficult and interminable: the interpretation of such moments is revisited and renewed again and again. We can never (completely) know the unconscious.

In practical terms, educators can do four things. First, instead of rushing through quantities of readings and content, educators can slow down the pace, encourage learners to identify their complex and contradictory responses to what is happening, and deliberately make time for learners to work through these responses. Rather than always pushing on to something new, we can cycle back through experiences and texts we have already worked through: examining these with fresh insights, comparing our current responses with our past reactions, and pondering the changes in our selves and our views. Second, educators can pose questions inviting learners to listen carefully to their internal responses, and share observations about their own internal conflicts. Questions can focus on contradictions in things said, on different feelings that seem to be expressed or undercurrent, on speculations about why particular events are emerging in the group. Third, in group dialogue or other learning activity, educators can mirror back to the group what they notice about how individuals are speaking and acting, and invite reflection about what these observations may indicate. Finally, educators need to attend to the multiple identities at play. Lisa Loutzenheiser (2001) urges us to actively interrupt the identity assumptions being made about one another among a community of learners: "Students have to feel as if teachers welcome them to a space of complex and contradictory possibility" (p. 214).

ROLES FOR PROMOTING RESISTANCE
TO DOMINANT NORMS
(Critical Cultural Perspective)

In critical pedagogy processes, learners trace the politics and come to critical awareness about their contexts. Critical educators view their role in varying degrees of radical politics as promoting this analytical process, as well as helping groups to generate strategies and actions for social justice and inclusiveness. One key pedagogical task, besides bringing together learners and questions about taken-for-granted conditions and policies, is to stretch and challenge learners' critical analysis. Another, for some, is to lead insurgent action. To this end, educators engage learners in inquiry about the justice and equity of existing

conditions, and encourage people to see links between personally experienced yearnings, conflict, and identity struggles, and
larger forces such as historical cultural dynamics and ideologies.
They ask questions about learners' as well as their own contradictory investments and implications in what knowledge counts
in particular communities. They push themselves and others to
become more aware of their own positionality and privilege,
their own investments and desires in a situation, and how these
might actually be contributing to the perpetuation of certain
injustices, inequities, and other undesirable conditions.

Educators also help others become alert to know how difference is perceived and enacted. They draw their own and others' attention to how images and words act to represent and
construct reality in particular ways, and how these may be taken
apart and constructed differently to produce more sustainable
or life-giving realities. Critical educators also continually revisit
their own pedagogical practice asking how development is measured, who gets to judge whom and why, and what interests are
served in the short and long term by their development initiatives. Within these general activities, critical educators tend to
adopt roles such as problem-poser and social activist.

Problem-Poser

Paulo Freire (1970) urged educators to engage people in
dialogue, to name their oppressive experiences, then rename
them in a process of transforming themselves into empowered
agents of social change. This problem-posing helps people to
come to consciousness, viewing as problems those inequities
and authorities repressing their lives that they have come to take
for granted as natural and inevitable, and viewing themselves as
actors that have helped sustain but also can resist repressive
forces. Educators play a vital role assisting people to read their
experiences and the structures and discourses that shape them.
But, beyond merely a cognitive activity of critical reflection,
educators help people to name and resist inequities, work collectively to change their own circumstances, and seek alternate

possibilities to the status quo of discrimination, racism, and sexism for more democratic communities. Specific approaches are outlined in Chapter 6.

Patti Lather (1991) urges educators to help people see the possibility for multiple readings of any situation, understanding that some readings are accessible and some are not. Like other feminist poststructural writers, Lather criticizes some of her colleagues espousing critical pedagogy (such as Henry Giroux and Peter McLaren) for lack of attention to their own fallible perspectives and their overemphasis on emancipating others through critical reflection. She advocates "a praxis that attends to poststructural suspicions of rationality, philosophies of presence, and universalizing projects" (p. 6). She exhorts educators to ground their thinking in concrete instances of liberatory pedagogy, but also to constantly question their own veracity, authority, and workings of desire in their practices towards freedom.

Social Organizer

Through critical pedagogy, groups of people and their values that have been lost or dislocated in rigid narrow identity categories recover and name new subject positions. It must be understood, in terms of this book's focus on experiential learning, that although critical pedagogy is often situated in classrooms it is also largely acknowledged to unfold in multiple nonformal sites of learning (i.e., consciousness-raising groups, movements of social activism, even individual confrontation with texts that disrupt one's received views). People learn to see through accepted social discourses to discern blurring borders and categories, new hybrid knowledges emerging, and even ultimate incommensurabilities of different cultural practices and groups. Giroux (1992) writes that critical pedagogy can open spaces to discern new futures, craft new identities, and seek social alternatives that may be obscured by current dominant ideologies and struggles.

At the end of the day, awareness-raising is only as good as the perspective of social change and the practical actions it engenders towards realizing that change, according to Finger and Asún (2001). In their vision, the best alternative to "learn our way out" of the crossroads at which adult education is currently stuck is through grassroots social movements. Their examples of radical feminist collectives, environmental, lesbian/bisexual/gay/transgendered (LBGT), antipoverty, and literacy movements are all characterized by resistance to existing conditions while building community alliances to develop more sustainable social alternatives. The educator's role is within and among these groups, assisting with clarifying, organizing, and strategizing.

But in practical terms, to what extent can a professional adult educator undertake the role of social activist or organizer? Despite educators' sympathies with social justice and desires to fashion a practice enabling adults' learning through social action, they may be inherently unable to enact such critical cultural practice. Tom Heaney (1996) argues that the professionalization of adult educators has subjugated their practice to the marketplace, and to its purposes of providing other professionals with knowledge and skill to sustain their claim to disproportionate wealth and power. Thus, concludes Heaney, to ensure their own continued existence, (professional) educators cannot truly support or even understand the fight for social justice carried out by front-line activists. Perhaps this is an unfair generalization. But the fact is that most social change movements seek de-institutionalization; authentic participation in them is difficult indeed for educators whose vocations are bound up with institutional goals of self-reproduction.

ROLES FOR ENHANCING
ECOLOGICAL RELATIONSHIPS
(Complexity Theory Perspective)

Turning to ecological perspectives of experiential learning, the educator is challenged to find modes of assisting learning that aim for precisely opposite effects. Rather than attempting to instigate change through problem-posing, renaming, and organizing, educators seek to open spaces for the system to experiment with change itself. Recall Dennis Sumara and Brent Davis (1997) who describe how systems of cognition and evolution interact in spontaneous, adaptable, and unpredictable ways that change both, resulting in "a continuous enlargement of the space of the possible" (p. 303). In other words, people participate together in what becomes an increasingly complex system. New unpredictable possibilities for thought and action appear continually in the process of inventing the activity, and old choices gradually become unviable in the unfolding system dynamics. Each participant's understandings are entwined with the others, and individual knowledge co-emerges with collective knowledge.

Educators plan starting points or disturbances to introduce into a system of learners, then watch carefully. They watch subtle particularities being created through myriad interactions in the system, amplify or make space for these, and remove barriers. Educators can also help all participants to see their own involvement, and seek honest ways to record the expanding space and its possibilities. To perform this role adequately educators need to become alert to a "complexified awareness . . . of how one [individual] exists simultaneously in and across these levels, and of how part and whole co-emerge and co-specify one another" (Davis & Sumara, 1997, p. 120). In more specific terms, educators promoting ecological relationships may undertake roles as interpreters and story-makers, as tuners[2], and as intentional participants in complex learning systems.

Interpreter and Story-Maker

The educator's role is first that of interpreter. The activity is assisting participants to name what is unfolding around them and inside them, to continually rename these changing nuances, and to unlock the tenacious grasp of old categories, restrictive or destructive language that strangles emerging possibilities. Second, the educator as story-maker helps trace and meaningfully record the interactions of the actors and objects in the expanding spaces. Educators help all to make community sense of the patterns emerging among these complex systems, and understand their own involvements in these patterns. Naturally, educators must be clear about their own entanglement and interests in the emerging systems of thought and action. Questions for facilitators are offered by Sumara and Davis (1997): How does one trace the various tangled involvements of a particular activity in a complex system, while attending carefully to one's own involvement as participant? How can actors' and objects' trajectories of movement be recorded in a meaningful way?

In contexts of organizations, Margaret Wheatley (1994)[3] suggests that educators can assist the flow of experiential learning in these complex systems by tracking and showing the system's own evolutionary changes. They can introduce or draw attention to the system's disturbances that create learning potential, and help amplify these disturbances by focusing, naming, and highlighting their significance. Educators can provide feedback loops to a system as participants experiment with different patterns leading out from disequilibrium. Finally, educators can help members of a system through the overall messy process they are experiencing in disequilibrium. Educators can help others to track the emerging patterns, to forestall the urge to contain and control, and to work creatively together through the disequilibrium to a new state of self-organization. Specific approaches are described in Chapter 6.

Tuner

Irene Karpiak (2000) has worked with complexity theory in thinking about her practice as a teacher in higher education. Although she doesn't directly describe herself as an experiential educator, Karpiak writes about "the emergent classroom" and its activities in ways that are clearly focused on experiential learning. For Karpiak as for other complexity theorists, learning is both gradual evolution through simultaneous integration and differentiation, and an expansion of the repertoire of possibilities incorporated by a system. Disequilibrium of the system is the prime motivator of learning. The teacher's role is central, but not necessarily as the stimulator of the disequilibrium. Rather, the teacher helps attune the learner and the learning community to the disturbances: drawing attention to the new possibilities created, while helping to divert patterns that may start to create unsafe spaces or power inequities. Karpiak's model of the teacher's role extends this central attitude of attunement to three values. *Communication* involves continual attentiveness and judgment, attuning to which of the many emerging possibilities and learner contributions should be amplified. Educators can provide positive feedback loops to amplify particular changes or threats in various parts of the system. *Contingency* is the only predictable condition in classroom practice that a teacher can rely on, so Karpiak suggests that the educator's role is to expect it, enjoy it, prepare for many possibilities, and attune to learner activity imaginatively. *Connectedness* refers to the educator's responsibility to help the classroom connect its parts to the whole system—individual learners to the learning community and its creations, the classroom community to the larger systems with which it interrelates, and learners to the inner parts of themselves.

Intentional Participant in Learning Systems

In their model of social learning showing how people learn new attitudes through dialogue in relationships with others holding very different views, Joke Vandenabeele and Danny Wildemeersch (2000) suggest four roles that people can take. One is the role of facilitator, when someone introduces a community or individual to a person with views that may challenge their own. A second role is that of obstructionist, which attempts to shut down the communication between people with different worldviews. Third is the role of broker, taken up by anyone who goes between two communities holding different meanings of reality. The fourth role, core actor, is someone who helps create a meaning that is taken up by a community. Which might an educator take up most profitably?

In different situations, an educator might assume any one

of these four roles. Presumably an educator interested in critically confronting learners' views will act as facilitator, introducing texts, questions, and people into dialogue that challenges prevailing definitions. In some occasions of situative learning, such as community development or workplace learning, an educator might act as broker or introduce someone else into a community to take on this go-between role, helping to link two groups with different interests and understandings. Where group members, whether in a classroom, workplace, or community, are struggling to develop new understandings of an issue, to reframe a problem, to adopt new habits among themselves, or introduce new terms into their language, an educator might assist. As core actor, an educator might amplify certain events and meanings, provide reminders and checks, or introduce vocabulary. Finally, an educator might sometimes need to play the role of obstructionist, disallowing views that may be destructive to the group's purposes or fragile new learnings. Vandenabeele and Wildemeersch (2000) themselves conclude that in cases where adults are learning through experience in public debates, such as those related to environmental or political issues, educators have important roles to play in helping to define these social problems, intervening in conflict when different views reach a deadlock, and reframing dialogue and relationships towards learning purposes. Most of all, educators can stimulate people to experiment with new proposals and meanings in their ongoing experiences.

CONCLUSION

While this chapter has presented distinct roles for educators as if they are fixed within particular perspectives and contexts of experiential learning, of course they are far more fluid. Real-life educators are pragmatic adaptors and integrators. Examples abound even in the theoretical world of mixed-mode pedagogical approach. For example, Cope and Kalantzis (2000) offer a pedagogical model that combines roles for educators as facilitators of dialogue, prompters of critical reflection, coaches and mentors, and environmental designers helping create opportunities for learners to participate in everyday problem solving and project creation immersed in a community. Wilma Fraser (1995) synthesizes four principles for facilitators of experiential learning that integrate insights from different theoretical orientations. First, suggests Fraser, borrowing from psychoanalytic notions, facilitators must engage with the problems inherent in the ways that our multilayered selves engage the world. Second, drawing from critical cultural orientations, Fraser suggests that learners should be assisted to examine the nature of experiences for the broader discourses that inform them—and construct them. Third, Fraser emphasizes that facilitators must acknowledge the power dynamic of the reflective process. And finally, Fraser reasserts her fundamental belief in the importance of learning through reflection on experience by stating that facilitators need to remember that new experiences actually occur in the process of reflecting on old ones, as old assumptions interact with new language, generating emotion (p. 41).

At the beginning of this chapter, Table 5.1 drew together threads of Chapters 5 and 6. Divided into the five perspectives of experiential learning discussed throughout this book—constructivist, situative, psychoanalytic, critical cultural, and ecological/complexity models—the table distinguishes common purposes animating educational intervention in experiential learning, and sets out the various possible roles for educators. Once again I caution that such a table is only useful as a way of representing at a glance the general topics of this chapter. In stark list form, these educator's "roles" belie the messy ambiguities and blurrings across the boxes that reality brings. These divisions are altogether too misleadingly tidy and ultimately too arbitrary to be useful as actual guides for practice. They are intended solely to provide a point of departure for the reader's own thinking and creative integration of rich new possibilities into practice. The final column of the table suggests specific activities, educational designs or plans, and learning occasions that might be associated with each of the five learning perspectives. This list forms the substantive content of the next chapter, where approaches for practice are discussed in detail.

NOTES

1. Heron (1992) suggested that experiential learning occurs in four modes: (1) learning through doing, (2) conceptualizing through language, (3) learning by imagining and intuiting, and (4) learning by encounter, which is "affective immersion" in experience.
2. Writers using complexity theory talk about enabling attunement: that is, educators help others attend carefully to their own and others' alignment with patterns emerging in a system.
3. Margaret Wheatley can be characterized as a practitioner and popular writer in organizational development approaches drawing on the "new science." Her work represents a simple introduction to these concepts. For further understanding, educators should consult the originators of general systems theory such as von Bertalanffy (1971). Other helpful resources in this area for educators include Capra (1996), Casti (1994), Prigogine (1997), and Waldrop (1992).

CHAPTER 6

Now What? Approaches for Educational Practice

Although very different pedagogical roles are suggested by different theoretical orientations in experiential learning, their descriptions here have been kept sufficiently open-ended to allow readers to imaginatively adapt and blend these roles in different contexts. The strength of this approach, however, is also its limitation. Open-ended generalities inevitably leave us asking, But what does this look like?

So this chapter provides specific examples, in the shape of activities and approaches for practitioners that are suggested by the five different theoretical orientations developed throughout this book: the reflection-on-experience orientation of *constructivist orientations*, the notion of participation in communities of practice of *situative orientations*, the focus on desire and interference-by-unconscious of *psychoanalytic orientations*, the resistance to norms towards social transformation of *critical cultural orientations*, and the co-emergent *ecological orientations* of complexity theory. The examples are listed in the same sequence in which they appear in Table 5.1. Although the examples are grouped to indicate certain theoretical allegiances, these classifications are very rough indeed. They should be viewed more as an organizing tool than as a theoretically reliable taxonomy.

The examples are highly selective, intended to offer brief sketches rather than a manual. The breadth across five theoretical orientations necessarily limits depth. Therefore although a setting is indicated in which each approach was developed and used (classroom, community education or workplace), this list still suffers from its lack of rich contextualization. Each approach depends very much on the detailed story of how it was used, by whom, amid what particular historical and cultural dynamics, and what kinds of dilemmas. Space consideration precludes these stories. Nor are the ideas presented in cookbook fashion as a blueprint for practitioners. As most educators know, using someone else's pedagogical strategy is tricky despite detailed instructions because everything changes according to the particular mix of people, purposes, and politics.

CONSTRUCTIVIST ORIENTATIONS

Adventure Learning

Adventure activities are becoming increasingly popular in leadership education and team development. The facilitator designs a sequence of concrete problem-solving challenges, usually set outdoors or in other settings where participants are separated from written texts. Groups of learners work together to solve the problem. These might be specific challenges of risk taking such as caving, scaling a mountain, negotiating river rapids — or participating in extreme activities such as fire walking and bungee jumping. Other experience-based training has borrowed from a long tradition of wilderness education, engaging participants in challenges of group survival or going solo: orienteering, finding food, and making shelter. Games created outdoors are yet another approach, such as trust falls, blindfolded walks in pairs, or a popular game in which a group must move each member through spaces in a rope web without touching the ground or rope. Purposes of these varied activities tend to focus on building trust, cooperation, commitment, and confidence among group members, as well as forcing people to deal with fear, uncertainty, and the need to develop a solution when lacking expertise and easy tools. In all of these forms the facilitator often creates the problem situation and provides the tools, sometimes observes the group's process, and usually leads a discussion during or after the exercise to help learners reflect on what happened and why, what choices they made, what strengths and weaknesses they discovered, and what lessons they learned. The power of the experience itself rests in a combination of high stakes and low competency, where people are compelled to rely on their own on-the-spot inventiveness and discovery of each other's non-routine talents.

Anthony Richards (1992) describes four phases to an adventure-based model of experiential learning, such as the Outward Bound program for young adults. Phase 1, Separation, involves preparing to leave the security and comfort of home behind to embark on an expedition. Phase 2, Encounter, is the most exciting and fully engaging part of the experience. The adventure is generated through meaningful problems that learners own and must solve through invention, usually in a context of perceived high risk. Phase 3, Return, involves reflection, consolidation, and story-telling, where learners begin to make connections between wilderness metaphors and home. The final phase, Reincorporation, leads adventurers to pursue the next challenge.

Proponents of adventure activities believe the challenge and unusual setting engage and motivate learners; supposedly increase people's risk taking, communication, productivity; and help increase people's insights into barriers into their team processes. Popular in management and organizational development activities, the wilderness in adventure education is assumed to function as an apt metaphor for the organizational environment. However, purveyors in training and development of outdoor education report the difficulty of assessing in any reliable way the learning outcomes of such adventure programs and their impact on individual and organizational effectiveness. Meanwhile safety and liability issues are always a concern in high-risk activity. While these problems may be uppermost for organizations trying to justify the return-on-investment for training, educators may be more concerned about the potential for adventure education to be completely commodified as frivolous novelty. More troubling questions have been raised about the personal and political consequences of a collaborative man-

aged adventure on workers and their organizational relationships in the return phase.

Environmental Education

A procedurally related but ideologically different approach
to integrating adult learning with experiences of the outdoors
is environmental education. The main distinction from adventure-based training is that instead of using the outdoors as a
resource, packaging it into sufficiently risk-posing activities
to stimulate adults' problem solving, environmental education
seeks to reintegrate people with nature, both for socio-environ-
mental change and human empowerment. As Darlene Clover
and her associates (2000) explain, this approach encourages
people "to re-connect with the rest of nature" as a site for learning with its own intrinsic value, and to explore human/Earth
relationships critically (pp. 4–5). One example they offer in a
practical sourcebook for environmental educators is entitled
"Learning through natural and community landscapes: dialogue with the rest of nature." Participants go out walking in
pairs, noting all the things they can feel, hear, and smell and
deciding whether these things are positive or negative parts of
the socio-biological community. Through dialogue, participants
analyse the environmental maps they have created, exploring
their reactions, and examining ways to enhance the positive and
reduce the negative elements for a healthy community.

Problem-Based Learning

Problem-based learning or PBL is widely used in professionals' education in medicine (Bligh, 1995), education (Casey
& Howson, 1993), pharmacy (Fisher, 1994), psychotherapy
(Aronowitsch & Craaford, 1995), and other disciplines. Casey
and Howson (1993) explain the goal of problem-centered methods as developing "creative, independent problem-solvers able
to harness their creativity through organization and planning"

(p. 361). The process of learning unfolds through the application of knowledge and skills to the solution of "real" problems in the contexts of "real" practice (Bligh, 1995). Problem-based learning typically organizes curriculum around a series of cases, each presenting a dilemma of practice. These cases are usually prepared in detail, researched, and based on an actual situation. Learners read, diagnose, and discuss the case, exploring strategies for analysing the issues and taking action on the problems. Problem-based learning is often acclaimed in terms such as "active, self-directed" and "student-centered" (Mann & Kaufman, 1995), encouraging cooperative, reflective, critical student engagement.

For example at Royal Roads University in British Columbia, whose graduate program in leadership begins with five residential weeks of PBL, the problem case is presented by an organization currently experiencing it. Learners are provided some briefing in the problem and its background and some instruction in problem analysis strategies, problem-solving approaches, communication, and reflective self-assessment techniques. Then in small groups they have one week to research, analyze, and prepare recommendations about the problem. Facilitators provide resources and questioning probes to assist the problem analysis, and offer frequent feedback on the group's problem solving and team communication. At week's end, groups present their solutions to the organization's senior management, and the entire process is repeated the following week with a new group.

However, PBL is not without its critics. Issues raised include the artificial, predetermined, historical nature of problems that students work with, placing them in a decontextualized space which occludes important political and cultural issues of situated professional practice (Fenwick & Parsons, 1998). Existing literature on PBL tends to focus on student achievement and methods of implementation (Aronowitsch & Craaford, 1995). How this achievement is measured, what professional perspectives are shaped by framing practice as problems to be solved, and what criteria are brought to bear on questions about what counts as meaningful knowledge for professionals, are less well-explicated (Fenwick & Parsons, 1998).

Project Learning and Classroom Laboratory

Project-based learning is usually more than simply assigning a field project to learners to complete for an assignment. Rather, it involves structuring a curriculum around projects that the learners formulate. This point is what distinguishes this approach from PBL: participants choose and take responsibility for completing a concrete project that is authentic (similar to or driven by an actual work task requiring completion, not necessarily related to a problem). In the process of working through the project, participants must solve practical and philosophical problems. The project might be developed in the classroom, such as a piece of art or imaginative writing that each participant chooses to design and develop day after day within the allotted class time. Or, the project may be external, something that each participant works on outside the classroom laboratory such as a research study, a change, or a program that the learner is implementing in a workplace or community context.

The classroom is turned into a laboratory offering resources such as books, concrete models, teacher-modeled strategies, and coaching and feedback from co-learners and facilitator. Learners solve problems emerging from their own practical project through a variety of means: trial and error, observing models, learning new strategies, accepting responses, and reflecting on the problem-solving process. The classroom thus provides both support through a collaborative community and distance from the participants' accustomed culture of practice, which helps them explore creative new worlds. But what the classroom chiefly offers are conversation and a safe place to assist participants as they work through difficult learning in each phase of their projects. *Personal conversation* promotes critical reflection on experience and feelings; *intellectual conversation* promotes comparison of theoretical perspectives and connection of these with various experiences of doing the project; and *dialogic conversation* offers a mode of exchanging responses and building stories and ideas with others. Throughout her book *Interwoven Conversations*, Judith Newman (1991) explains her own strategies as educator within an experiential learning laboratory she created with her graduate students:

- Help learners identify consequential problems and effective strategies for examining issues and completing tasks.
- Build in choices wherever possible by asking such questions as: What issue do you want to pursue? What's a way you could pursue this interest? How will we select issues to address as a group? How are we going to conduct this discussion?
- Acknowledge learners' feelings of confusion, uncertain direction, and being overwhelmed.
- Allow learners to work through these feelings to find their own direction, refraining from rescuing but also intervening when a learner is truly stuck.
- Frequently draw attention to the facilitator's own motives, underlying beliefs, and goals, and critically monitor facilitator-participant interactions.
- Continually monitor learners' progress individually through the problems raised in their project work and through their connection-making with their own practice: probing for deeper thought, challenging risk, validating process, confronting assumptions, and juxtaposing new points of view.

Most important perhaps, learners are nurtured through the struggle of personal change occurring in a project involving transformative learning. The premise here is that the insulated classroom laboratory offers time and space to discern the emerging problems of the project and practice new strategies that will transfer when participants engage in similar real-world projects bounded by practical limitations.

Coaching Strategies

Clearly coaching is important in all of these approaches focused on reflection upon challenging experiences. Donald Schön describes the role of coach in detail in his influential *Educating the Reflective Practitioner* (1987). The coach provides encouragement, asking, Where does it go from here? The coach also draws attention to strategies the student already knows or can observe from fellow students and other models available to them, shares personal experiences and encourages other learners to do the same to show the universal commonalty of problems they experienced, and demonstrates alternative strategies to achieve the desired effects. Above all, coaches must help learners accept that learning takes time.

Schön (1987) introduces three coaching strategies to help novice practitioners develop not only prescribed skill levels but also the ability to creatively problem-solve and critically reflect on their problem approaches. In "joint experimentation" the coach works alongside the learner to suggest different ways of solving the problem, trying the proposals together, and talking through the consequences of these actions on the problem itself. In "follow me!" a learner imitates that coach's actions as closely as possible, repeatedly, while the coach prompts the learners to articulate what they are feeling, thinking, and resisting. In the "hall of mirrors" approach, the teacher urges juxtaposition of as many points of view as possible. When no conflicting perspectives emerge or when early consensus is reached, the teacher raises issues and nudges learners to link these to practice. Each story they tell becomes an opportunity to probe: Why do you remember this? What makes it significant? What do you learn from it? What is one question it raises for you about your practice? The coach in essence holds a mirror to the learner to question the learner's constructions of reality, while simultaneously mirroring the coaching transaction to assess and make new decisions about the process of guiding. Occasionally the coach must confront a learner reluctant to enter the looking glass, shaking existing beliefs loose from familiar meaning perspectives, and thus creating the discomfort necessary for critical reflection. Judith Newman suggests that coaches be continually on the alert for critical incidents (what some call teachable moments). She asks adult learners, What just happened here? How did you respond? Her objective, like Schön's, is helping learners develop a meta-awareness of their interpretations and responses to the moment of experience.

Mentoring

For Lois Zachary (2000), mentorship is a longer-term coaching process in which both mentor and protégé grow, learn, and reflect critically through an engaging relationship. As mentors, educators help people to identify their learning needs in work, find self-directed learning opportunities, and support the learning process. Mentors can help learners create a learning plan with clear goals, criteria for success, responsibilities, definitions of accountability, and protocols for addressing problems encountered in carrying out the plan. They can provide support by encouraging and affirming the learner's choices, challenging the learner's assumptions, re-orienting learners to their original visions and goals, and helping learners generate various options when they get stuck. Mentors also can help mentees make problems more manageable: putting into wider organizational perspective what may appear to be overwhelming problems, and developing longer-term views of the consequences of their actions. Zachary's (2000) book *The Mentor's Guide* sets forth practical suggestions for negotiating the terms and boundaries of the mentoring relationship, providing clear, focused feedback without overwhelming a mentee or imposing the mentor's style and view of the problem, and bringing the relationship to a satisfactory end.

The advantage of mentorship is the one-to-one assistance with specific real-work issues, enabling exploration of multiple layers of complexity and contradiction. Usually the relationship extends over time, so a bond of trust develops which often can enable both partners to challenge one another. The disadvantages include the time involved and the possibility of mismatch in personal style and expectations of the relationship. Greater issues unfold at the philosophical level, where mentorship often stops short of critically examining values and power structures in organizations, including the power hierarchy embedded in the mentorship relationship. The mentee is constructed as an individual bent on self-development, at worst patterned after the mentor's developmental view of expertise, whose learning is separated from processes of the community of practice and its discourses. Furthermore, mentorship models tend to divert attention away from consideration of important influences wielded by organizational networks on both mentor and mentee.

Reflecting Critically on Work Experiences

Critical reflection in the workplace enjoyed a surge of popularity in the 1990s as organizations rushed to become exemplars of continuous learning. The notion was that if all workers could be trained to challenge their own mental models or taken-for-granted assumptions about how to do things, and reframe the problems they found themselves facing repeatedly, the organization could become more productive. Peter Senge, one guru of this learning organization genre, and his associates recommend a variety of approaches for critical reflection in *The Fifth Discipline Fieldbook* (1994). One activity they suggest is "Five Whys," where a problem is analysed by asking five "why" questions at successively deeper layers to get at root causes (pp.108–112). In "Undiscussables" members of a group anonymously write down underlying unmentionable issues troubling the surface discussion, which can then be analysed by the group to reveal power relations, root causes, and fears (p. 404). In "Multiple Perspectives" different stakeholder roles and viewpoints in an issue are clarified, then participants take turns adopting these as the group works through problem-identification, analysis, and responses (p. 273). "Moments of Awareness" invites participants to stop and reflect whenever they feel frustrated by what is happening around them, or are surprised by the results they get:

> What is happening right now? (What am I doing, feeling, thinking right now?) What do I want right now? (What am I trying to achieve in this activity or conversation?) What am I doing to prevent myself from getting what I want? Say I choose to . . . Then take a deep breath and do it. (p. 216)

This is an example of helping people to reflect-in-action, to catch themselves in the midst of what David Beckett (2001) calls hot action, to pause and test their assumptions and choices.

Critics argue that, as in mentoring processes, without attention to issues of power, equity, and justice these approaches leave untouched an organization's basic structures, leadership, reward system, staffing processes, and contradictions between philosophy and procedure (Fenwick, 1997). Without examining these structures and relations of power, critical reflection becomes rehabilitation for the employee who carries the burden of organizational problems constructed as training issues. However this critique, important as it is to illuminate the tendency to domesticate critical reflection, should not obscure the liberatory potential of people examining their experiences with a critical and historical eye.

SITUATIVE ORIENTATIONS

Service Learning

Service learning is an approach based on authentic situated concrete experience where people "learn and develop through active participation in thoughtfully organized service experiences" (Kinsley & McPherson, 1995, p. 126), sometimes combined with guided critical reflection. Traditionally service learning programs are planned for youth or postsecondary students, as a supplement to their schooling. The experiences are often community-based volunteer work with different nonprofit organizations such as elder care, wildlife refuges, inner-city centers and the like, and typically organized for a short-term period of a few weeks. The service work is usually integrated with study. For example, Florida State University (Easton, 2000) offers a course called "Learning in the Community" using a service learning model. Prior to the service activities (30 hours in an agency picked by each learner), a group of participants are coached to learn about their chosen organization's functions, philosophy, and constituents; to examine its service needs; and to propose their own potential role. Participants are gathered together periodically throughout the service term to share reflections on their experiences, assess their contributions and the relationships they are forming, and develop approaches to enhance their effectiveness as service providers. They keep a reflective journal throughout the program, and complete a project at its conclusion assessing the values and limitations of the experience for themselves, the agency, and the community needs served. Advocates claim that, overall, service learning offers powerful educational experiences where "interest collides with information, values are formed and action emerges" (Kinsley & McPherson, 1995, p. 9) in developing practical skills as well as a sense of citizenship. Young people are reconnected to each other and to their communities as they participate in building civil society.

However, Janet Eyler and Dwight Gilles (1999) have suggested that participants are sometimes dumped into organizations with little opportunity to participate in challenging learning activities. As peripheral drop-ins to complex systems, they are often constructed as individuals in projects that essentially use them for cheap labour. Furthermore, argue critical writers, service learning permeated with liberal notions of self-actualization do little to build civil society when there is no structural critique of the social conditions creating the needs the service attempts to address. Roger Boshier and Dave Harre (2001) describe an alternative example in New Zealand where facilitators actively challenge learners to expose and deconstruct the contradictions and exclusions they experience during the service work. Roger Simon and colleagues (1991) at the Ontario Institute for Studies in Education offer similar examples of applying critical pedagogy to service learning in their book *Learning Work*. They suggest that teachers help students actively critique the conditions of work they experience, the power dynamics in the social relations they participate in, the criteria used to determine what counts as competency or good work, and the inequities and resistances they observe.

Designing Situative Learning Environments

While service learning approaches situate learners directly in authentic activity, others have experimented with designing environments or activities in the classroom that simulate actual conditions. Working from principles of situated cognition, John Seely Brown and Patrick Duguid (1993) suggest that teachers can design environments that convey tacit but important knowledge:

> It is a fundamental challenge for design—in both the school and the workplace—to redesign the learning environment so that newcomers can legitimately and peripherally participate in authentic social practice in rich and productive ways—to, in short, make it possible for learners to "steal" the knowledge they need. (p. 11)

In formal education settings such as classrooms, the environment can be designed to simulate an apprenticeship, using simulations, use of video, online interactive narrative situations, and other techniques to create authentic contexts with multifaceted problems that learners must identify and work through (Cognition and Technology Group at Vanderbilt, 1990). The educator designs challenging tasks requiring creative engagement, exploration, and diverse approaches. The environment should provide people with technical assistance, opportunities for trial-and-error and practice, time to internalize the learning, and help to develop self-monitoring and self-correcting skills. The challenge is avoiding the natural tendency to present learners with already-framed problems, stripped of other complex pressures, politics, and relationships of authentic practice. One example is a school principalship simulation offered at the University of Alberta where graduate students assume the role of principal in a particular school for the duration of the course. In the labs, students work through an in-basket of long-term and short-term tasks, while confronting unexpected dilemmas presented through telephone calls and video clips. In class debriefs students receive feedback on their responses from practicing school principals, reflect on their practice, and analyse the embedded issues in their simulated leadership.

Such approaches may obscure the essential point that a simulation is still artificial, and situated within the politics, purposes, and relationships of classroom formal learning rather than an authentic workplace. Therefore facilitators might encourage learners to identify elements of the classroom situation shaping their responses and experience in simulations and to analyse the sorts of knowledge they are developing within that situation.

Cognitive Apprenticeship

One specific form of combining designed simulated environments with direct assistance has become known as cognitive apprenticeship (Brandt, Farmer, & Buckmaster, 1993). This involves five phases. Phase 1, modeling, provides a demonstration *in situ*, along with a verbal description of the activity as it is being modeled. In phase 2 learners approximate the model of action and think-aloud description, with supportive coaching and scaffolding assistance to bridge the gap between observing someone else and developing complete independent competence. In phase 3, fading, the coaching and scaffolding are gradually reduced, moving learners to phase 4, self-directed learning, where assistance is only provided when requested as learners continue practicing independently. Phase 5, generalizing, focuses on assisting transfer of the newly developed competence. Alternate applications and modifications are demonstrated and discussed, with reminders to learners to try the competence in new situations.

Cognitive apprenticeship moves away from a purely situative view of learning, treating learners as independent reflective constructors of knowledge. However, the strong connections binding learners to their environment (the coach and the activity in which demonstration and scaffolding take place) are stressed. One example is offered by Mike Rose (1999) who studied the training of physical therapists in simulated situations in classrooms alternated with field experience. Rose stresses the important role of instructors who interweave a wide range of approaches and an ecology of representations that surround the situated activity with talk. Instructors repeatedly demonstrate, use models, tell experience stories, create metaphors, and call up textually derived knowledge of anatomy and biomechanics. As students practice, instructors talk through the learners' efforts, guide, remind, correct, and physically adjust learners' actions. Gradually the instructors fade not only their own instructional props but also the different scaffolds built into the learning process (learners vocalizing their sensations as they perform actions, drawing diagrams representing the movements they were attempting to reproduce, and working with partners to achieve desired results). In this fashion learners gradually become independent, internalizing a repertoire and getting the feel of practice.

Action Learning

Moving away from designed to naturally occurring situative contexts, action learning based on writings of Reg Revans (1980)[1] has become enormously popular in workplace organizations, proliferating in a growth industry of action inquiry technologies. In action learning, individuals tackle priority problems and dilemmas that are often complex and messy, under actual conditions, where history offers no solution. Learning is assumed to be context bound, with change-based data, purposes, and value choices, and dependent on the nature of people's participation. Through a form of critical reflection, people are encouraged to bring underlying assumptions to consciousness and reframe those assumptions that don't accomplish desired goals. Facilitators help people identify the problems, and accept responsibility to take action on a particular issues through a process of unlearning and relearning (Dilworth & Willis, 2003). A small group or set of about six people, all experiencing the problem as real and compelling, work through the action learning process. Colleagues support and challenge each other in the process of resolving the problems through group data analysis and data mapping, conjecture and refutation, advice and support, collective attention to governing values, group generation of action strategies and their consequences in a case, and group critical reflection at every phase of the process. The entire process integrates research to illuminate what is felt but not evident, with action to improve a situation and reflection to question insights.

Victoria Marsick and Judy O'Neil (1999) show that the projects chosen for action learning should be meaningfully linked to both the organization's objectives and the individuals' needs. Participants need time granted to work through both the action and reflective dialogue phases. Project sponsors or facilitators within the organizations are recommended to help guide and support the project, and mediate the group's work with the organization's goals, politics, resources, and philosophies (Adams & Dixon, 1997). Facilitators can guide groups to focus on analysing the problem or developing a solution. Research by Simon Priest and Michael Gass (1997), both consultants in the use of experiential approaches for corporate training, tried to determine which approach was most effective in workplace settings. They found that for functional corporate groups, either approach was equally effective. However, when working with what they define as dysfunctional corporate groups, problem-focused facilitation was less effective while solution-focused facilitation was extremely successful at encouraging teamwork.

These understandings presume that action learning is situated and transformative (in that it challenges past practice to frame new problems and solutions). However, it does not fundamentally resist or reconfigure prevailing organizational structures of inequity, or address the contradictory power relations that may obstruct genuine empowerment of individuals in work organizations.

Direct and Indirect Guidance in a Community of Practice

An alternative to this reflective learning process focused upon an extended workplace problem is to enhance everyday learning opportunities in a community of practice. Stephen Billett (2001) shows ways for educators to enhance learning through what he calls direct and indirect guidance. *Direct guid-*

ance involves informational resources or colleagues demonstrating, answering questions, creating relational links, and in other ways assisting the community newcomer to gradually move into full participation. *Indirect guidance* involves arranging opportunities for the newcomer to observe and practice participation. These may include assigning varying tasks and work groups; enlarging individuals' scope of responsibility; allotting time for learning, reflection, and dialogue; and moving people to different sites and projects of activity. Indirect guidance is useful for helping people develop the ability to make practical judgments, or nonroutine decisions that are highly context-sensitive and provisional. David Beckett and Paul Hager (2000) suggest how on-site workplace educators might help create access to opportunities requiring practical judgments within the social and political norms of a community of practice. For example, people need opportunity to engage in complex situations where they must judge what the problem is, as well as opportunity to make judgments that have direct meaningful impact on the organization. Educators can enable individuals' opportunity to make a series of intermediate judgments prior to the final or culminating judgment, to assess their consequences and adjust their framing in changing organizational circumstances. Educators can also ensure access to support, technical information, and trial testing with experienced others as individuals develop practical judgments.

Billett notes that without educator intervention, learning "affordances" of a workplace community may be inequitable or ineffective: coworkers may be unwilling, unavailable, or unskilled in guidance; opportunities may be denied to certain workers on the basis of class, race, gender, or community status; necessary learning time may be overridden by greater value placed on production defined as doing and output. Educators can examine particular environments for their learning affordances and constraints. They can raise issues of equity regarding workers' appointment to special projects and positions with greater scope of responsibilities, and the availability of travel/observation opportunities to encounter new sites of culture and activity. Perhaps most important, educators can emphasize the

need for time. People need allotted time to experiment and in-
novate, colleagues need allotted time to provide direct guidance,
and the community needs patience for the lapsed time required
to absorb new members, new knowledge, and changes to practice. Without this emphasis, too often learning is subsumed into
production where it is quickly forgotten in overloaded task
schedules and pressures.

PSYCHOANALYTIC ORIENTATIONS

Encouraging Reflective Autobiography

As noted earlier, autobiography appears to have become a
popular approach among adult educators interested in making
spaces for learners to revisit and interpret their personal histories of life experience in a deep way. We have seen the work of
Pierre Dominicé (2000), who developed a guided educational
biography process. Working in small groups where rapport and
trust have been developed, people share oral narratives of their
learning experiences often organized according to a focus such
as developing a particular competency, understanding their
commitment to their occupation, or examining their schooling
lives. As they tell and retell these stories, listeners and facilitators may guide through questioning, inviting the narrator to
probe root meanings, connect recurring themes, and explore
small moments or missed stories. Through the process people
try on different interpretations of their stories as they also listen
to others' ways of telling and making sense of their life experiences, until they are ready to write their educational biography.
The entire process is, of course, a highly interpretive act mediated by the language and values of the situation and community.
Madeline Grumet (1992) reminds us that watching the dynamics of a performing self through a reflective autobiographical
process is by no means a simple act of recollection:

> To what extent does reflection, even when subjected to rigorous
> discipline, distort experience to fit idealized forms? Does the dis-
> tancing required by the phenomenological perspective break the

bonds of commitment and action that tie us to the real world? Who is the self that we attend? Is the reflecting self continuous with the acting self? Do our multiple social roles splinter the self into situational poses strung along a temporal chain? (p. 40)

Playing with these different stances (the observing-I, the I-in-situ, the not-I) and different roles (narrator, character, subject), Warren Linds (2000) opens the possibilities of writing autobiography. He demonstrates writing a past-lived experience as a scene in script form in one column, interposing present reflections on its meanings and future speculations on its significances alongside the scene. Or, a written narrative of experience can be transformed into a poem by gathering key phrases and images, and playing with their rearrangement on a page.

Linden West (1996) describes gathering learners in groups to generate and share autobiographies, partly motivated by West's belief that many people struggle to find coherence and meaning in a world that is increasingly threatening and stress-ridden. Through collaboration, people find ways to name what is difficult to say or articulate, and to think about its meaning collaboratively. This process strives to surface power relationships, discomforts, dead ends, and uncertainties. West is a psychologist, and draws upon psychoanalytic theory as well as cultural theory in forming his approach: projecting inside oneself the images of "good others" with whom one's inner self can interact in positive relations, and with whom one can experiment imaginatively with different ways of being. A more confident self-image positioned within wider cultural scripts emerges from these internal interactions. The entire process helps develop an openness to others' support as well as more fluid, creative responses to crisis and change.

Multiple Text Readings

As explained in Chapter 5, some psychoanalytic perspectives of learning suggest that reflective processes—as well as teaching-learning interactions—are shot through with unconscious dynamics that are difficult to access through rational analysis. Mark Bracher (1993) suggests a method of interpreting texts through various readings to encourage deep listening to one's own (both teacher's and student's) largely unconscious desires and resistances. The first step is finding a text sufficiently powerful to engage learners' energy and emotions, such as a provocative image, story, or film clip. Then, educators assist learners to each attend to and share their own responses, and map the resulting "identities" that the text produces in themselves as subjects. Learners are encouraged to listen to where their response is ambiguous, paradoxical, or resistant—in other words, where they find themselves refusing understanding. Then through subsequent dialogue, the educator can help draw forth these responses to bring unconscious fantasies and fears to voice. Often these challenge culturally approved symbols, images, and identities. Bracher explains that the transformative work is to identify, alienate, and separate desires from currently accepted "master signifiers" (culturally approved symbols, institutions, and images) to produce new master signifiers that can change the fantasy and desire embodied in the subject. It is only through examining lesser signifiers that any movement towards change can occur. That is, Bracher explains, educators can help people to examine and perhaps find expression for those alternative desires that may lead to new productive identities and action alternatives.

Educators must carefully consider group dynamics of power relationships and authority structures that prohibit such dialogue. The classroom is a charged political space. Psychoanalytic workings-through must be broached with exceeding caution to avoid invasion of private spaces, associations of the confessional, presumptions to control through knowing subjects, issues of transference, and multiple inequities.

Confronting Difficult Knowledge

Deborah Britzman (1998a), also using psychoanalytic learning theory, brings the focus back to the educator's own reflective work. She suggests that educators attend carefully to their own educational biographies, seeking in particular those

contradictions, ambiguities, and love-hate conflicts in their learning and practice. Educators deal "in repression, denial, ignore-
ance, resistance, fear and desire" when they teach (p. 70). Britzman suggests that we examine those sites of our own resistance
to knowing, the dark shadows of our fears and guilt within our
practice interacting with learners. In general, theoretical work
exploring intermeshings of difficult knowledge with pedagogy
is rich and complex, irreducible to technique.[2] Nonetheless,
some reflective approaches have been suggested to assist this
process. Free-association writing begins with describing everything that can be remembered about a troubling incident and
continues unedited scrawling without stopping, often evoking
layers of contradictory thoughts and feelings. Then the narrative
can be scanned to locate an uncanny moment or curious feeling,
and a new piece of free-association writing focuses just on exploring this moment or feeling. Photo memory-writing begins
with a compelling photograph of oneself, writes everything
recalled about the situation of the photograph from within its
moment, then writes about the moment as history interpreted
through lessons from all life's interceding experiences. Found
poetry writing works with personal text such as a journal por-
tion or other piece of one's writing, and creates a poem from
selected phrases in a way that helps capture the voice or voices
that can be discerned within the text. Photographs or collages
to represent one's desires or repulsions, drawings of one's river
of life or tree of knowledge create text that helps prompt reflection on inner drives and recurring patterns.

   This becomes a pursuit and recovering of "lost subjects"
that "haunt education in the form of its contested objects: as
conflicts, as disruptions, as mistakes and as controversies" (p.
19). When educators make known their own self-conflicts and
how these are manifest in their pedagogy, they learn to tolerate
difficult knowledge and the difficult workings-through that students experience in coming to confront their own conflicts.
While educators are not psychoanalysts, we can examine traces
of our own unconscious desires (for certain knowledge, for students' love and identification with them, for authority) in our
actions and responses. In undergoing this analytic process, we
may be more likely to provide spaces and support for learners

to work through their own resistances and ignorances, and less likely to repress these conflicts as insignificant or illusory.

Decoding Workplace Language and Environment

According to Mark Bracher (1999), one helpful function of workplace education based on Lacanian psychoanalysis is to help clients become aware of the "master signifiers" and images that dominate a given organization, the way people's identities are affected by these, and the conflicts or suffering these signifiers cause. For example, if poor work is criticized as timid or productive performance praised as bold, then bold becomes a master signifier representing something ideal, to be desired and reproduced. If aggression in organizational relationships appears to be causing problems, perhaps underlying forces causing people to identify with boldness is partly responsible. In terms of visual-spatial environments, Bracher explains that we continually scan our environments to nourish our egos, our own sense of bodily unity and coherence. Some people feel reassured by wide-open well-lit spaces, while others feel disoriented and threatened, preferring to be surrounded by personal objects in small spaces. Size, climate, lighting, colour, obstacles, and access to windows can produce anxiety, depression, and ego fragmentation or a sense of well-being and even power. In terms of desire, Bracher shows how people project their desires for fundamental pleasures onto other people, objects, and interactions. For some, this might mean nurturing and protecting a talent that makes them invaluable to an organization or another person. Some derive profound gratification from fighting the system. Some work themselves sick for approval, finding pleasure in being desired by others; others work for magic rewards — solving an impossible systemic problem, climbing ever higher on a career ladder, aiming for profit margins or other goals that are always set just out of possible reach.

The psychodynamics of these experiences can be decoded, a process in which the learning involves identifying the psychological forces and assuming responsibility for them. The educa-

tor facilitating this process can work at the micro level, with individuals, or at the system level, with the organization. Learners
can find alternative ways to express and act on their repressed
desires, or learn to sublimate and displace destructive impulses.
They can confront and work through anxieties caused by images,
words, and environments at work. Alternatively, an organization can learn to identify how its environments and signifiers
may be enhancing or threatening individuals' sense of identity
comfort. People can be involved in a process of decoding these,
and together redesigning work goals and tasks, rearranging fur-
niture and other environmental aspects, or introducing new signifiers to develop other dispositions of psychological forces.

Understanding One's Desires and Anxieties in Work

In workshops that he conducts, Mark Bracher suggests the
following exercise to encourage individuals to examine deep-ly-
ing desires and anxieties operating in their vocational lives and
learning. To each of the following questions, write your responses rapidly and without stopping to think or edit. Write
down as many details of the external and internal experiences
associated with these prompts as you can remember:

1. Why did I decide to become a _____ (or, to enter
   _____ work)?

2. What was my most pleasant (frustrating, exciting, humiliating, joyous, satisfying, engaging, inspiring, uncomfortable,
   disappointing, etc.) experience?

3. What was my most anxious (proudest, unpleasant, fulfilling,
   depressing, etc.) moment?

Of the above, choose the most significant positive and
negative experiences and flesh out the details-people, environments, events, and interactions as well as internal feelings,
thoughts, and interpretations. Analyse the experiences by asking questions like these: How did I try to capitalize on or generate these positive aspects in other experiences? How did I try

to avoid or repress these negative aspects in my other experiences? How did these experiences affect my identity? What recognition or validation did I receive in the positive experience? What recognition did I desire but not receive in the negative experience? How were others affected by these events? In what instances did I pursue my identity needs to the detriment of others? Then shift your analysis to exploring more productive alternates: What other practices could help me meet my identity needs? What other master signifiers could link my identity needs with others' needs (or organizational goals, or my own vocational objectives, etc.)?

This sort of internally focused analysis may be chosen by an individual, or usefully adapted by a group to reflect upon a process experienced collectively. However, there is real danger in imposing such a reflective activity upon others in workplace environment, where such invasion of privacy in a high stakes environment is manipulative and unjust. Furthermore, without thoughtful consideration exercises like these can distort complex psychoanalytic processes into empty, technical nonsense — as Bracher's critics have pointed out.

CRITICAL CULTURAL ORIENTATIONS

Facilitating Problem-Posing

Critical cultural writers urge educators to go much further, to critically assess and challenge unequal relations of power. This is different than critical reflection, which focuses on analysing one's individual assumptions, and moves to social critique. The process is problem-posing (Freire, 1970), introduced in Chapter 5, a group learning process to help people confront their experiences in terms of how power structures work and what can be done towards social change. The process begins by naming the issues of concern in people's lives, then finding information that can help identify general causes and outcomes of these issues. For example, union educators Mike Parker and Jane Slaughter (1994) offer exercises for leading worker groups in critical examination of their experiences. In one activity the group collectively brainstorms management's goals, then the means used by management to achieve their goals, then union goals, and finally various means or tactics used to achieve union objectives. Participants are guided in finding any overlaps between the two lists of goals and means, the circumstances where overlap occurs, the reasons for switches in tactics, and the underlying patterns linking the two lists.

The *Resource Manual for a Living Revolution* (Coover et al., 1993) suggests a fairly systematic approach for facilitating the group's problem-posing dialogue. It begins with a process of identification where the facilitator is responsible for organizing and observing the group as they identify shared themes in their experiences, then proceeds through steps of codification, making the theme into a problem, and decodification or problem solving. Throughout, the facilitator coordinates activity, listens and prompts analysis in dialogue, challenges participants' thinking, and guides the process of assessing problems and exploring solutions. However, more radical educators like Paula Allman (2001) have criticized such approaches for domesticating Freirian critical education, turning it into an instrumental system that bleeds the politics and passion needed to motivate and sustain the difficult undertaking of radical social change. Recall Griff Foley's (1999) arguments, outlined in Chapter 3, that the most powerful critical learning happens through collective social action. Astrid von Kotze (2000), explaining the urgent needs for critical adult education in South Africa where she works with communities, returns us to the power of dialogue and the natural flow of social action from participatory learning processes within a reflective framework of questioning and probing:

> Listening to returning refugees sitting in the dust of a village square as they relate tales of survival under conditions of drought and political strife is both a humbling experience for educators, and an ennobling one for villagers who are dignified by the respectful listening and ensuing action based on their knowledge. [But] such listening should lead to discussions on how local problems related to other issues in a broader way, how they are linked

to systems and institutions. This is what Freire meant by assert-
ing that it is impossible to "discuss, to study the phenomenon of
life without discussing exploitation, domination, freedom, democracy, and so on." (p. 167)

Jennifer Gore (1993) appeals to critical educators to be,
above all, rigorous in their own self-examination. Educators
must carefully scrutinize their motives and desires, and the real
consequences of engaging people in problem-posing and its so-
called emancipatory dialogue. They need especially to continually question the authority of their own position as the good
liberator. Gore cautions educators against the tendencies to impose their own grand visions for people's lives, or to essentialize
and simplify people's experience in the process of critically ap-
praising it. A commitment to remain personally wide-awake and
critically conscious in a society of stupefying consumption is a
continuously difficult endeavor.

Popular Education

Popular education, based on Freirian problem-posing approaches, is typically a community-based process. As Liam Kane
(2001) describes it, popular education is distinguished by its political analysis and commitment to the oppressed. Branches of
popular education have developed in areas of human rights,
community development, gender, basic education, indigenous
peoples, popular economics, health education, justice, and peace.
As with action learning in the workplace described earlier, the
facilitator's role is to help group members identify and assess
what they have experienced as recurrent problems in their communities. But unlike action learning, facilitators of popular education help link these to larger socio-economic forces and power
dynamics affecting the community's well-being, then plan and
take action towards changing their responses to these forces.
Darlene Clover and her associates (2000) suggest the following
considerations for facilitators in the difficult process of popular
education: discovering the value of patient prodding rather than

goal-seeking and clock-watching; permitting silence and having the patience to allow the participants to ponder, think, and squirm; admitting (and knowing) one does not have all the answers; and taking risks even with possible outcomes of error (p. 33). Kane (2001) points out that popular educators are more interventionist than facilitators: they promote a dialogue of knowledges but are explicit about their ideology and intentionally provoke political engagement.

In popular theatre (Prentki & Selman, 2000), one particular approach to popular education, participants are guided through a series of exercises to explore unresolved conflicts and embedded problems in their concrete, real-life experiences. They improvise sociodramas to portray these, then analyse causes and links to broader social forces. For example, people may be invited to create a series of still tableaus representing events related to a particular issue. These tableaus can be brought to life, interrupted and analysed, or changed by substituting invented characters and alternate choices of action. Or groups might improvise a problematic situation that the others stop periodically to examine critically and make suggestions for action, which the group incorporates by dramatizing hypothetical scenarios and consequences of possible choices. One character portrayed in an improvised scenario might be isolated from the scene and invited to answer questions about personal motives, feelings, and responses from those watching. Invisible theatre or street theatre presents a scene designed to promote debate in a nontheatrical public venue. Like any approach to popular education, popular theatre must be carefully planned and thoughtfully facilitated. The group must be sufficiently prepared through rapport-building and preparatory exercises. Time and space considerations must be arranged to allow participants to develop comfort with the process and work through its challenges.

Critical Learning Through Social Action

Many critical-emancipatory educators argue that without action, there cannot be learning. Armchair critical analyses supposedly do not generate the praxis, the integration of action and reflection in an ongoing dialectic that produces transformative learning. Critical adult educator Griff Foley (1999) writes, "some of the most powerful learning occurs as people struggle against oppression, as they struggle to make sense of what is happening to them and to work out ways of doing something about it" (pp. 1–2). His book is full of case studies around the world showing that people's personal experiences of social action—involvement in actual struggle between insurgent and dominant discourses—is central in their critical learning. The nature of this emancipatory experiential learning is not developmental in a linear progressive fashion, nor is it inevitably triumphant in terms of enabling personal and collective liberation. Michael Welton's (1995) caution about critical learning in social movements is important to remember: while they have the potential to foster generative forms of communication, moral insights, and emancipated thinking, their forms do not necessarily produce "enlightened, empowered and transformative actors" (p. 26).

The process of learning, observes Foley, is *conscientization*, the coming to awareness of one's own implication in one's oppression that Paulo Freire (1970) describes. Foley contends that this process is not an individual psychological change, but is embedded in a community of actors. First, the initial participation is sparked in a gradual community awareness of the need to act. Second, the learning process is entangled with opportunities for collective action, the ways people come together, the spaces that emerge for this transformed consciousness to flourish and formulate action, and the ways the community develops an activist discourse. Third, much of the significant change is people learning connections between them: recognizing the universality and solidarity of their lives, while learning their diversity of experience and ideology (and how these differences could be exploited by others). Fourth, significant learning is embedded in their activity and not articulated as learning by the people. Fifth, emancipatory learning is not cumulative but embedded in conflict, and develops in unanticipated ways. The learning itself is as continually contested, complex, ambiguous, and contradictory as the struggle between dominant and insurgent forces.

The actual knowledge people learn through social action experience, according to Foley, is self-confidence, critical understanding of how power works in society, and the resources and flexible process required in direct action. They learn the need to support each other, the nature of the stress involved, how action can polarize a community and reveal its structures, and how unsettling it is to challenge your own and others' assumptions. Their learning demystifies how authority works, and helps them appreciate people's very different perspectives and the extent of their reconcilability. Perhaps the most important knowledge is people learning that they *could* act and that their action *can* make a difference.

Recent studies of global social movements suggest questions we need to continue to ask about learning through social action (Holst, 2002[3]; Keck & Sikkink, 1998). What, for example, triggers the sense of oppression or exploitation in ways that motivate different individuals in a movement towards conscientization? And what are the different forms of conscientization that people experience in social action? How and why, exactly, do different kinds of action become formulated from these varying points of cognitive or moral dissonance? Finally, where do different individuals find themselves located at different points in the social action/learning process? Social movements provide rich sites for exploring the complexities of experiential learning, ranging from communal resistance to individual rights groups, from local solidarity to transnational advocacy networks.

ECOLOGICAL ORIENTATIONS

Open Space, Future Search

From an orientation of complexity theory, two approaches have been advocated to encourage experiential learning in communities. Open Space was originally developed by Harrison

Owen (1997) as an approach to assist a particular community to surface and pursue its own issues requiring dialogue. The guiding principles are these:

1. Whoever comes are the right people.

2. Whatever happens is the only thing that could have.

3. Whenever it starts is the right time.

4. When it's over it's over (duration is determined by the dialogue, not pre-determined time allotments).

5. The Law of Two Feet. People can leave to join a different dialogue according to their interest.

   Participants are asked to think of an issue related to the focus of the meeting for which they feel some energy and are willing to take some responsibility as group leaders. Each person who has an issue to bring forward briefly explains this issue to the others in the circle. The issues are given titles and posted on pieces of paper on the walls. Participants are given time to sign up for issues attracting their interest. Group leaders then find a room for discussion. People go to these rooms and share observations. Group leaders take notes and ensure that participants head back to the plenary room at the completion of the discussion. Results are shared, and the group decides next steps.

   Future Search is a similar loosely structured approach to enable a community to move collaboratively towards helpful dialogue.[4] The difference is in purpose. While Open Space helps issues emerge, Future Search is intended to help create a common vision, identify desirable/undesirable practices as defined by the community, and define values for a desired future. The community focus in a Future Search is not solving problems, but developing insights, understanding each other, raising commitment, uncovering new possibilities, and reducing misunderstanding. As many constituents as possible in the community, including various internal and external stakeholders, are invited. The process varies, but often includes the following three movements conducted by an entire community, assisted by a facilitator:

1. Examine the community's history. Identify different views and meanings found in successful and unsuccessful events, good and bad trends, weaknesses and strengths of guiding principles, and the values and actions shaping the community's direction.

2. Identify external events and trends affecting the future.

3. Generate concrete images for a future, collectively considered to be the most desirable and attainable actions for self, unit, and organization.

Educators assisting a Future Search offer no diagnosis of problems, no prescriptions for fixing things, no preconceived issues, and no frames of reference or action ideologies. They "don't judge information as good or bad, complete or sketchy, useful or futile, appropriate or redundant. Whatever people do or say—their words, their behavior, their wishes, and their reactions—belongs to them," write Marvin Weisbord and Sandra Janoff (1995). Not knowing what issues and obstacles will arise, facilitators simply set a workable process in motion and let the system develop its own meanings and motivation. In short, they help participants self-organize.

Clearly this approach of helping dialogue emerge in a community differs fundamentally in educational purpose from the critical social action approach presented earlier, where the facilitator is exhorted to help the community link its experiences to larger forces perpetuating exploitation and inequity. However, the two approaches are not as dichotomized as they might appear. Both ascribe to the learning power of dialogue about, and enmeshed with, collectively experienced action. The extent to which an educator might introduce ideological critique is influenced by contextual factors:

- The strength of the community and its identity.
- The readiness of individuals for social critique and political action.
- The nature of those felt problems with which the community most identifies.
- The commitment of individuals to these issues.

- The extent to which people feel more tightly or loosely affiliated with the community.

As we move to contexts of workplace practice where educational purpose is highly contested, we see similar considerations driving the particular approaches chosen to promote learning through experience in work.

Disequilibrium, Amplification, and Feedback

Recall that according to ecological learning theory, disequilibrium experienced in one part disturbs and gradually changes the whole system, especially if it becomes amplified and communicated to other parts. Feedback loops assist the system to self-organize by detecting, selecting, and creatively adapting itself to new patterns emerging within itself. However, what appears to be messiness in this process often induces an impulse to create controls, boundaries, and structures that actually suppress and choke the flow of creativity. Educators can introduce or draw attention to the system's disturbances that create learning potential. For example, strategies suggested by the Plexus Institute (2001) for creating organizational "noise" might include highlighting the different attitudes among people in a work group (not to create conflict but to encourage members to recognize and use the energy of these differences). Or educators can deliberately encourage people to try going "the wrong direction," doing things in unexpected ways, or taking "foolish excursions" now and then to see where they might lead. Educators can be alert to and help amplify random or serendipitous disturbances and paradoxes in an organization by naming and highlighting their significance.

Because learning is co-emergent there is little certainty or use in trying to plan a grand direction for learning through a work project. So, educators can help encourage workers to try several small experiments simultaneously, reflect on what happens, adopt "good enough" vision rather than cling to rigid arbitrary standards, and gradually shift their time and attention towards those experiments that seem to be working best for the time. Educators can also provide feedback loops to a system as it experiments with different patterns leading out from disequilibrium. They can show, for example, how the processes unfolding in multiple experiments at the fringes of an organization reflect patterns going on in the larger system—just like the single leaf reflects the pattern of the whole fern. Finally, educators can help members of a system through the overall process they are experiencing in disequilibrium. They can be helpful in tracking the emerging patterns, showing others how to watch for authority changing from person to person and knowledge fluctuating as new understandings emerge in small corners. They can help others forestall the urge to predict and contain, becoming more flexible and adaptable; and working creatively through it to self-organization.

Occasioning

Turning to classroom practice informed by complexity theory, recall that Irene Karpiak (2000) wrote that the teacher's main role is to help attune learners to dynamics that are not readily apparent. This approach is somewhat aligned with the psychoanalytic focus on the uncanny outlined earlier. However it is rather less invasive and certainly less focused on the internal psychic worlds than on the relationships between internal and external elements of various systems at play.

Davis, Sumara, and Luce-Kapler (2000) use the term *occasioning* to explain how classroom teachers might think about their role as enablers of learning in a complex system. Because complex engagements such as learning involve "adjustment, compromise, experiment, error, detour and surprise," teaching is really occasioning in that "things and events fall together in complex and unexpected ways" (p. 144). The teacher's role is not to control the process, but to help enact occasions where learners go about adapting activities, responding, performing, playing, improvising, planning, and varying. For example, adapting occasions are those where a teacher may instigate a flexible task, then follow student leads as they adapt and interpret the task for themselves. Playing occasions are those important spaces where a teacher might offer a focus and learners are encouraged to experiment freely with possibilities—such as ideas for interpreting a phenomenon, solutions to a puzzle, alternate ways of creating something, and so on. Varying occasions are based on a principle of complexity theory that a healthy social system is marked not by homogeneity, but by diversity. It celebrates its members' specializations in diverse interests and talents. The teacher who believes this, therefore, does not impose all the rules, roles, procedures, and expectations. This does not mean that there is no structure or plan, however. But a classroom activity plan need not be a step-wise carefully controlled procedure. The approach of occasioning suggests that the teacher provide a focal point, suggest a purpose, and encourage learners' engagement in one or more specific ways (adapting, responding, performing, playing, and so on). The emphasis is upon enabling choice and specialization, and upon ensuring a classroom space where diverse skills and approaches are embraced—not just by the teacher, but also by the community of learners.

Organic Structures

In ecological perspectives of learning, classroom structures are necessary, but certainly not in rigid or technocratic approaches. When classroom activities are considered in more complex terms, organic structures can be seen as necessary conditions for learning and creativity: such structures enable possibilities while simultaneously limiting them. This balance between freedom and restraint that spurs learning is what Davis, Sumara, and Luce-Kapler (2000) call "liberating constraints":

> Well-crafted learning activities are ones that maintain a balance between enough organization to orient students' actions and sufficient openness to allow for the varieties of experience, ability and interest that are represented in any classroom . . . The idea

of selecting and writing about a button is one possible example of such liberating constraints. The writer focuses only on one button but can write about any memories or connections that she or he realizes in that writing. (p. 87)

So when thinking of classroom structures as liberating constraints, experiential learning plans should not map out a route of activity. Instead, structures may consist of a specific point of focus that provides a departure for learner activity, or perhaps a general goal that allows many paths to its end point. Besides flexibility and relinquishing control of the steering wheel, which are critical teacher characteristics in this approach, two more teaching dimensions are important to achieve the balance between constraint and liberation in such organic structures. First, teachers must think carefully about the context of learners' engagement when deciding an activity: How might time of day, location of activity, availability or restriction of resources, external events, learners' own expectations, and the specific mix of learner personalities affect the energy and possibilities of their engagement? Second, teachers need to be gifted in working through the actual moments of the teaching/learning activities: following/stimulating the energies of the group and individuals, as well as enhancing the possibilities as they open up moment to moment. This suggests that teachers need to be creative improvisers—listening for possible leads from learners, helping people link possibilities and build on them, and restraining their own desires to control the proceedings or rescue learners from puzzling-through things on their own. It helps when teachers have confident familiarity with the concepts and skills being explored, and personal experience with the activity in which they seek to engage learners.

The notion of liberating constraints in planning and facilitating can be applied to almost any activity suggested for experiential learning in this chapter. That is, almost any activity—from fire walking to project-based learning—can be controlled through a teacher-map that strangles possibilities and ultimately, learning. Conversely, almost any activity—from contemplation of a single object to immersion in complexity—can be undertaken in ways that expand the space of possibilities and liberate learner freedom, creativity, and critical thinking.

The examples for practice described here are not always commensurable, and the discussion here in no way intends to adjudicate the various approaches. The final judge of any practical approach must be the educator, who is the most intimately familiar with his or her own pedagogical style, philosophy, and context of work. As such, educators can and do integrate different perspectives and approaches in particular learning communities—each characterized by unique relationships, intentions, meanings, and constraints.

The intention here is simply to plant seeds for those of us who are practicing educators—starting points to spark our own creative thinking about alternative pedagogical interventions. But we are yet in danger of wreaking violence in the name of strategy—a word that, after all, derives from the Greek *strategos* which literally means to plan the destruction of one's enemies through the effective use of resources.[5] The relentless pursuit of pedagogical strategy—the more instrumental bits of this chapter—can reduce our teaching-learning relationships to technique, and learners to objects upon which our technology performs. What saves us as educators is remembering these relationships to be sacred, and our invitation to them as profound honor. How we respond to that invitation cannot be a question of "how" without a clear-hearted sense of our "why." This critical issue of our purposes for intervening in people's learning through experience is taken up in the concluding chapter.

NOTES

1. Much empirical research and practice have developed Revans's original ideas in various contexts. For mainstream approaches to action learning in contemporary organizations, readers may wish to consult Marquardt (1999) or a recent practical guide by Robert Dilworth and Verna Willis (2003). For critical approaches to action learning, consult Matt Alvesson and Hugh Willmott (1996).
2. Interested readers are encouraged to explore the recent work of

those working with psychoanalytic theory, learning, and education such as Derek Briton, Shoshana Felman, jan jagodzinski, Adam Phillips, Alice Pitt, and Judith Robertson besides Britzman, Bracher, and Ellsworth referred to in this book.

3. John Holst (2002) shows the wide differences among social movements in political commitments for social change, and the concomitant differences in learning potential, objectives, and learning processes. Old social movements are rooted in critique of the political economy: Marxist-inspired revolutionary struggles for a new order are developed according to working class or proletariat perspectives. New social movements do not focus solely on the working class or seek revolution to fundamentally transform political and economic systems. Instead they agitate around identities of difference (such as gender, race, sexual orientation) or issues beyond economics such as quality of life, peace, and clean environment.

4. The description of Future Search offered here is based on Weisbord and Janoff (1995).

5. So says J. Bracker (1980) in "The historical development of the strategic management concept," *Academy of Management Review,* 5 (2), pp. 219–224.

CHAPTER 7

What's Next? Further Research about Experiential Learning

This book has been developed as a response to three primary questions. First, what is the nature of the intersection between individuals, situation, social relationships, and knowing? Second, is there a legitimate role for an educator in this process? And third, where educators have an ethical role to play in experiential learning, what purposes and approaches should guide this role? The focus throughout has been on grounding these questions—thinking through the rationale, perspectives, and issues in experiential learning—rather than on prescribing strategic responses. The previous chapter's list of instructional approaches for practicing educators can imply a too-tidy closure on the complex questions we grapple with. So this final chapter returns to questions leading out from these three which, while perhaps leaving us less comfortable than we may wish, are surely the most authentic dwelling place for educators in these uncertain times.

MODELS OF EXPERIENTIAL LEARNING IN RESEARCH AND PRACTICE

First, when so much critical and alternate learning theory has been generated in the past decade, why is there so little evidence of its incorporation in applied research and practice of experiential learning? The individualistic constructivist model of David Kolb (1984) appears to have captivated educators and researchers. A bibliography prepared by David and Alice Kolb

(2000) show 378 journal articles and 130 doctoral dissertations from 1985 to 1999 basing research on Kolb's theory of experiential learning and learning styles. About half of these fall into the fields of education and management; the rest represent applications in higher education related to computer science, psychology, medicine, nursing, and accounting. For example, studies continue to validate Kolb's four learning styles in experiential learning, and to apply these to new contexts such as team process (Kayes, 2001) and entrepreneurs' learning (Begley, 2000). Other research links individuals' learning styles (as defined by Kolb's Learning Style Inventory) to their learning and performance in professional education, such as hospitality students' study times and test achievements (Bagdan, 1999); interior design students' visualization skills (Nussbaumer, 1998); and nurses' accuracy in ECG interpretation (O'Brien, 2000). In all of this, there appears to endure an uncritical acceptance of Kolb's bifurcation of concrete experience and reflective observation, and his claim that individuals fit one of four learning styles regardless of learning context, purpose, and individual's culture and development.

Incorporating Technology into Experiential Learning

Research and practice are also rapidly expanding the uses of *virtual environments* to create concrete experiences and stimulate reflection. Focus is on exploring new ways for technology to support rich experiences through animation, visualization, and simulation enabling learners' total immersion and interactivity (Pimentel, 1999). However, technology must be integrated with three other important elements in designing effective virtual learning environments: (1) various learning styles; (2) varied experiences for learning (demonstrations, discovery, problem solving, pleasure levels, performance level demands, and practice opportunities); and (3) varied environmental complexity (Pimentel, 1999). For example, *affectively complex* learning environments simulate what it is like to be immersed in a situation, or encourage learners to reflect on their experiences to generate these insights and feelings themselves. *Perceptually complex* learning environments help learners understand new concepts or problem-solving processes, perhaps by presenting different perspectives or requiring different modes of interactions. In *symbolically complex* environments, learners must solve an abstract problem for which there is a best solution by analysing data, applying rules, and drawing on informational databases. In *behaviorally complex* learning environments, the emphasis is on responding to a practical "real-life" problem.

These dimensions appear useful for thinking through design of experiential learning opportunities in face-to-face settings, and virtual environments can offer imaginative experiential opportunities that are impractical or unsafe for novices in real-life scenarios. However such models of computer-based learning, by themselves, manipulate learners and learning processes. They focus exceedingly upon learning as a rational exercise, and present experience as isolated from fundamental dimensions of bodily, psychic, cultural, and social engagements.

Educational Practice in Experiential Learning

In both the workplace and professional education, experiential pedagogical practice appears to be dominated by Kolbian approaches based on inducing novel experiences followed by facilitated reflection. Applications of *adventure-based learning* are common in corporate training as well as therapeutic uses. In psychiatric treatment, for example, ropes courses and other adventure-based approaches have enjoyed popularity for behavioral therapy (Gass & Gillis, 1995). The area of *games and simulations* has also grown, particularly in corporate training. The Society for the Promotion of Games and Simulations meets annually to share strategies for developing games, and research continues to examine the effectiveness of simulations for helping learners develop and apply concepts in higher education (i.e., Herz & Merz, 1998). Initiatives for continuing professional education based on *action learning* also continue to hold appeal. For example, a new broad-based experiential learning program for health professionals across Canada combines evidence-based practice (using recent empirical research in clinical decision making) with learning projects and classroom instruction (ELP, 2000).

In higher education focus tends to be placed on testing the usefulness and most effective strategies of experiential pedagogical approaches (based on reflective constructivist models). Examples include ethical training for lawyers (Moliterno, 1995), cross-cultural learning for social workers (Boyle, Nackerud, & Kilpatrick, 1999), and doctoral programs in political science (Marando & Melchior, 1997). Experimentation with *service learning* (Delli-Carpini & Keeter, 2000) and *problem-based learning* (Colliver, 2000) continues in different fields of professional education, focused on either refining effective applications or raising questions about what, if any, are the learning "outcomes" of experiential approaches (Colliver, 2000).

For practicing adult educators interested in developing and promoting experiential learning, opportunities for information sharing are plentiful. At the time of writing, over two dozen major organizations devoted to experiential learning had websites. The International Consortium for Experiential Learning (ICEL) presents a large biannual conference and maintains a directory of experiential associations and groups. The Association for Experiential Education (AEE) serves practitioners in education, outdoor adventure programming, management development, environmental education, and recreation, and maintains forums for special interest groups (women in experiential education, lesbians, gays, bisexuals, and allies). The National Society for Experiential Education (NSEE) focuses on research and resource development for experiential education in formal education settings, particularly service learning, active classroom learning, and internship. The Council for Adult and Experiential Learning (CAEL) promotes access to experiential education through partnerships with business, government, labor and higher education. The International Foundation for Action

Learning is one of many networks promoting action learning for organizational development. Strong interest among groups devoted to assessment of prior learning experience or recognition of prior learning continues to be supported through conferences, assessment kits, and training courses offered through organizations such as the Experiential Learning for Assessment Network (ELAN).

These examples of practice and research demonstrate a growing acceptance of experiential pedagogy, and a commitment to promoting its liberatory potential for adult learners. But almost all still define and assess experiential learning in conventional terms, as immediate concrete experience followed by structured mentalist reflection, measured according to observable behavioral change. Where are the influences of situative, critical, psychoanalytic, and ecological perspectives of learning? Where are the deeper questions of context, power-knowledge configurations, psychic dynamics, communities, and systems in producing experience and determining what is understood as learning? These influences on mainstream educational practice appear to remain rather small, confined to pockets of radical activity and scholarly inquiry.

POSTMODERN STRUGGLES: LANGUAGE, POLITICS, AND UNDECIDABILITY

But in these pockets, challenging questions are emerging about reflection, power, conversation, and flexibility in the practice of experiential learning. Among those who have adapted and enriched the models of Kolb as well as Boud, Keogh and Walker (1996) is Nod Miller, a British adult educator who has worked extensively with experiential learning and autobiographical processes. She describes herself as attempting to situate these models of reflection upon concrete experience within postmodern and feminist perspectives, where things known are uncertain, identities are constantly shifting, and power relationships between people shape their learning together. Miller

(2000) tells about her own learning that reflective processes demand considerably more time, emotional energy, and personal challenge of adults than experiential learning models may imply:

> A formulation that I have found useful in structuring reflection is to address the following three questions: what happened, what did it feel like, and what can I/we learn from the experience? . . . In doing so, I recognize that I am to some extent attempting to impose a modernist rational sensibility on what often feels like a splintered and shifting reality. The experience of the postmodern subject is unlikely to fit tidily into the well-ordered categories and stages of the model outlined here; however, I am perhaps still enough of a modernist to seek to construct some order out of the uncertainties of my personal and professional life. (p. 79)

Her tale demonstrates the tightrope walk between a postmodern acknowledgment of fluidity and the human impulse to seek sense-making through structured reflection—an impulse that perhaps explains the persistent popularity of Kolb-type models despite 15 years of critique from alternative learning perspectives. Richard Edwards (1994) is one of these critics, claiming that most writing on experiential learning is "largely normative, i.e. arguing whether or not experiential learning is a good thing, or mechanical, i.e. how it occurs and how it can be improved" (p. 423). Yet Edwards goes on to argue that despite its historical casting within a liberal humanist paradigm, and its faulty assumptions about the autonomous self and experience being concrete, experiential learning actually shares many tenets of postmodernism. These include the relativism of knowledge, giving more status to knowledge constructed in everyday life; the attack on the notion of privileged canons of culture such as literature; and the shift from text to image, from detached analysis to immersion in experience. Finally, according to Edwards, experiential learning and postmodernism share acknowledgment that there is no single point of judgment for what is truth: both argue that what is right flows according to the vantage point of people immersed in the experience of a particular moment.

Some research on social networks is exploring how learning flows among people interacting and distributing knowledge among multiple nodes. While material texts may try to fix meaning across time and place, multiple voices and actors participate in these—adapting, accepting, appropriating, resisting, and perhaps disrupting their meanings. Bill Cope and Mary Kalantzis (2000) show how individuals' experiences of meaning-making within the languages of their environments may either open new pedagogical possibilities or present new systems of mind control and exploitation. They identify six "design" elements of the meaning-making process: linguistic meaning, visual meaning, audio meaning, gestural meaning, spatial meaning, and multimodal meaning (integrating combinations of sense-making). People must become fluent readers and speakers, engaging these meanings fluently in a particular community of practice. But more important, people must also learn to critically interpret, transform, and transfer to other settings these six designs of meaning. Cope and Kalantzis call this form of experiential learning "multiliteracy," and suggest a pedagogical framework for facilitating it (integrating reflective learning, situative learning, and critical learning).

Ironically Kolb (1998) himself, in extending his experiential learning model, has focused most recently on examining conversation as experiential learning. Meanwhile, some research continues to trouble the notion of reflection, and question the commonplace assumption that learning happens through sustained critical scrutiny of one's experiences. For example, Gordon Ball's (1999) study of transformative experiences among people who learned a commitment to global sustainability found that they did not recall any period of reflection as part of their transformation. While all could point to life-changing breakthrough experiences that were unfamiliar, fully sensual, and emotionally intense, any reflective activities happened "inconspicuously . . . perhaps even unconsciously, and in the context of everyday activities" (p. 261). Similarly Laurent Parks Daloz and associates (1996) found, through interviews with people who "learned" active commitment to the common good, that transformation developed not necessarily through reflection but embedded in encounters with others: over time these gradually evoked a sense of diversity and "consciousness of connection" (p. 215).

Patti Lather (2000) is among those interested in how language, audience, purpose, and identity make the reflective act itself an interpretive reading or even performance of remembered experience, rather than a realist representation of it. She writes about the "undecidability" of lived experience. What we think we see, when we reflect, "is always already distorted":

> [Remembrance is] less a repository for what has happened than a production of it: language, writing, a spectacle of replication in an excess of intention. Remembrance is not about taking hold but a medium of experience, a theatre for gathering information. (p. 154)

These insights help remind us of the folly of clinging to tidy formulas which would have us believe that learning is a straightforward matter of deriving lessons, clear to all, from our "true" memories of a "concrete" experience. First, these memories depend upon what truths are possible to acknowledge within the cultural values and politics of our habitats. Second, there are many slippages between the named and the invisible in our meaning-making. There are further disjunctions between the so-called learner and those other readers of experience who allot themselves the authority to do so under the title of educator. Third, concrete experiences are *not* isolated from other life experiences, from identity, or from ongoing social networks of interaction in the learning process.

As educators we may be too disposed to focus on those short-term time-bounded learner experiences within our own purview. Perhaps we need reminding how small and incidental educators' roles often are within the gradual layering of experiential webs that generate individuals' most-valued learning and change. Perhaps we could focus less on techniques of experiential learning and more on issues, Miller (2000) suggests in her postmodern treatment of experiential learning. What are the power relations between learners and promoters of experiential learning? How can emotional dimensions of learning be understood and responded to? What constraints are placed on experiential learning by the social, cultural, technological, and economic contexts in which learning takes place? And, what are its ethics and issues of negotiation and consent? (p. 84).

WORK, THE ECONOMY, AND EXPERIENTIAL LEARNING

These questions of power relations, emotions, constraints, and ethical pedagogical practice are particularly thorny in the workplace, where continuous experiential learning has become a dominant ideal to be encouraged and guided by educators in any way that will enhance workers' capacity. Studies of informal learning in the United States and even situated learning is increasing, exploring how in-the-moment learning is caught up in day-to-day experiences.[1] Few of these, however, acknowledge power and language dynamics shaping communities of practice. We have also seen the work of researchers such as Beckett and Hager (2000) and Billett (2001) in this area, who explore facilitative approaches and environmental design that can enhance situative learning. So-called learning organization initiatives attempting to convert workers into continuous experiential learners are popular (Senge et al., 1994). Complexity theory (Plexus Institute, 2000; Wheatley, 1994) is also currently fashionable for developing organizational productivity through learning. Meanwhile applied research continues to experiment with the so-called transfer potential of experiential learning for human resource development through wilderness adventures, spiritual camps, and the transformation of corporate managers into educators.

However, hot arguments rage between critical or labor educators and those aligned with human resource development over pedagogical purpose and ethics. Some tend primarily to support the organization's goals and definitions of worthwhile knowledge, linking workers' productivity to competitive advantage. Others fight for critical education in the workplace. Many have argued (Collins, 1991; Cunningham, 1993; Hart, 1992;

Kincheloe, 1999; Schied, 1995; Usher & Solomon, 1999) that
as general notions of experiential learning become increasingly
colonized by the category of workplace learning, educators are
adopting core assumptions of human capacity as capital resources, learning as commodity, and providers as market com-
petitors. Ian Baptiste (2001) is among those denouncing the human capital orientation of workplace learning (where
knowledge, attitudes, and skills are developed primarily for
their economically productive potential) for its "moral bank-
ruptcy." Baptiste shows that when aligned with human capital
theory, pedagogy becomes apolitical, adaptive, and individualistic. Focus on the technical, treating all learner needs as desirable, does not acknowledge serious conflicts of interest. Focus
on adapting people to their work environments ignores the social, political, and economic disparities creating the conditions
to which people must be continuously adapted. And focus on
the individual discourages collective analysis and action to
change these conditions and address fundamental problems.

Educators struggle with ideology, torn between allegiances
to client-managers and worker learners fighting for dignity and
quality of work life within the machinery of reengineering
(Cunningham, 1993), or between seriously conflicting interests
among groups of workers. As recent studies have demonstrated
(Salt, Cervero & Herod, 2000), even when worker-educators
agree that an international workers' education movement is
needed to challenge "the current hegemony of neoliberalism in
the TNC-dominated global economy" (p. 28), their solidarity
is split by deep ideological differences. Some align more with
accommodatory goals (workers learning to succeed and protect
their own interests within global capitalism) while others seek
more transformative goals (worker groups reaching beyond national interests in learning/acting together to challenge and
transform fundamental relations of global capitalism). Within
these ideological wars, educators collide with employers and
other interest groups to assert control of the discourses and activities of experiential learning, often pressured to reconcile
radically different goals with insufficient resources, little knowledge of each others' programs, and small trust of each others'

Name _____

Address _____

City _____

State: _____ Zip (+4) _____

Krieger Publishing Company
P.O. Box 9542
Melbourne, FL 32902-9542

We would like to keep you informed about other KRIEGER PUBLICATIONS

Please use this form to request future literature in up to four (4) categories.

Subject Categories

- ☐ Medical Sciences (C)
- ☐ Psychology/Sociology (E)
- ☐ Education/Communication (F)
- ☐ Anthropology/Philosophy (G)
- ☐ History/Religion (H)
- ☐ Engineering/Technology (J)
- ☐ Chemistry/Biochemistry (K)
- ☐ Mathematics/Statistics (N)
- ☐ Business Sciences/Economics (P)
- ☐ Biological Sciences (R)
  (Botany, Ecology, Zoology, Biology, Nature)

- ☐ Physical Sciences (S)
  (Geology, Geography, Oceanography, Water/Soil Management, Astronomy, Meteorology, Ecology, Environmental Science)
- ☐ Veterinary Medicine (V)
- ☐ Adult Education (W)
- ☐ Space Sciences/Physics (X)
- ☐ Public History (Y)
- ☐ Herpetology (Z)
- ☐ Other_____

Name_____

Mailing/Street Address_____

_____

Country _____ Postal Code/Zip(+4)_____

Tel:_____ FAX:_____

e-mail:_____

VISIT OUR WEBSITE FOR COMPLETE INFORMATION ABOUT KRIEGER TITLES AND MONTHLY SPECIALS
www.krieger-publishing.com

(100M) 11/00 directmail4up

interests. So the most compelling question of experiential learning perhaps is found not in the myriad conceptual and technical issues raised throughout this book, but in morality: What purposes ought to govern our continuing questions for inquiry and practice in experiential learning?

THE EDUCATOR:
ASPIRATIONS AND COMMITMENTS

Educational purposes in experiential learning are hotly debated around politics, ethical relations, visions of humanity, and faith in pedagogical solutions. Radical political commitments range from socialist to pluralist forms of social transformation. More liberal educators point out the ironies of democratically minded educators pronouncing what others should want and think. However, their critics hold that liberal educators' purposes have been coopted by globalized capitalism. When our practices as educators support an economic system that benefits the few at the expense of the many, ask radical educators, "what intellectual and emotional feats do we perform every day in order to erase from our consciousness the fact that 90% of all people are trapped in the struggle for daily survival?" (von Kotze, 2000, p. 171). Postmodernists argue that such fixed positions of identity and power do not exist in complex contemporary systems and discourses, and deconstruct the whole notion of meaning-centered rationality and so-called reflective practice. In reply, educators advocating radical challenge of social structures attack what they construe as postmodern refusal of pedagogical responsibility. Finger and Asún (2001), for example, claim that postmodern fragmentation and incoherence perpetuate anxiety and erode communities. Social exclusion and inequality continue, they write, precisely because grand narratives of domination and power are assumed not to exist by postmodernists, and educational or political projects for social change are rendered impossible by postmodern insistence on non-oppositions. According to Allman (2001), Marxist and Freirian educational approaches are enjoying a renaissance among educators interested in equity, social justice, and sustainable communities.

But as we saw in Chapter 4, not all radically minded educators support the critical educative stance of liberating people from their false consciousness and distorted ideologies. Michelson (1999), one of the most original voices in the arena of experiential learning, opposes altogether the liberatory gesture that she believes displaces people's actual experience by emphasizing rational critical reflection. Leading out from her alternative notion of "carnival," educators might seriously consider ways of helping people to explore the availability of widely diverse meanings within their cultures and societies. In particular, educators might encourage people to explore what Michelson (1999) calls "transgressive" meanings, those possibilities for action and identities that are often repressed, hidden, denigrated as deviant, disciplined, or otherwise kept contained from dialogue about human experience.

Michelson is not suggesting criminal or harmful activity, but recovery of those events emerging in society (and in our own memoried experience, our fantasies and dreams) that we tend to dismiss or sanitize. When these collective experiences are spotlighted and examined, they reveal repressed but honest energies circulating in our culture. They also open alternative meanings that may help expand our somewhat limited repertoire of what it means to be human. "Carnival" appears in many cultural sites of revelry and pleasure: think of celebrations and masquerades, initiation rites, parades, feasting, and sporting events. Transgression occurs, too, in those moments that break out within the everyday world of work, projects, and rational life—eroticism, rapture, ecstacy, pain, humiliation, the sacred, horror—and in which we lose ourselves. As Georges Bataille (1988) has described in his complex studies of inner experience, these vital moments of transgression are moments of loss, of small deaths. In each of these we as subjects are dissolved and returned as something new, having experienced a glimpse of the infinite other. Accepting our participation in these as important learning not only reconnects us with our bodily energies but affirms our very humanity and opens its possibilities.

Michelson's introduction of transgression to experiential learning theory also points to the significance of both play and art in human experience and learning. Play has been discussed by other adult educators (Melamed, 1987) as a way of generating new meanings and unleashing spontaneous creativity. Through play we explore ways to express our identity and relate to others. Because playful episodes give us permission to disconnect temporarily from narrowly rational and linear approaches to problem solving, they help renew energy and expand perspectives. Expressive art, as Peter Willis and his colleagues (2000) demonstrate, also opens new ways of playing with and performing various forms and voices that can illuminate complex dynamics of has been/being/becoming in experience and learning. Through aesthetic modes of experiential learning, adults might well find and animate expansive new visions of human freedom from alienation and exhaustion.

Other educators are also wielding a language of hope and possibility to replace pedagogies of control and management in experiential learning. John Field (2000) exhorts educators to consider how the very pressures of continuous innovation and permanent learning in which they are implicated are widening inequality and exacerbating market assaults on fragile environments and communities. In his vision for a new educational order, Field suggests strategies for educators to help increase individuals' social capital: raising the status of informal learning, extending its reach to those excluded and ensuring it is geared to the common good (p. 147); enabling individuals' participation in broader social and work-based networks; working for more flexible, modularized accreditation of individuals' experiential learning (p. 145); and continuing to democratize institutions that shape people's everyday experiences and learning (family, community, voluntary bodies, government institutions, and schools) (p. 150).

Finger and Asún (2001) argue for replacing the educational metaphor of developing people with one of participating with them—in projects, vision-making, and grass-roots movements towards sustainable communities. In particular Finger and Asún advocate for the recovery of Participatory Action Research, an adult education tradition, as a form of social learning through organizational change. They suggest strategies for educators to join with others in a three-phase process (becoming aware, clarifying conceptions, and developing alternatives) to counter what they portray as urgent threats to social ecology: turbo-capitalism, eroding politics, postmodernism, and ecological crisis. The overall point of all of these writers is that, given the centrality of experiential learning in people's lives, educators must be clear about their moral and political purposes justifying their involvement in others' experiential learning. For Field and others represented here, this purpose must have something to do with putting learning "at the service of a global development strategy that is economically efficient, socially equitable, ecologically sustainable and politically democratic" (Field, 2000, p. 155).

CONCLUSION

I have argued throughout this book that the learning perspectives selected for discussion offer fruitful insights and illuminate each other's shortcomings. As practicing educators fostering experiential learning we should, I believe, draw freely from their precepts and recommendations according to two things: the demands of our practice context, and our deepest sense of what we are called to do as an ethical adult educator within that context. This is not just a pragmatic stance but also a political and moral choice. Our first task is to be clear in understanding fundamental distinctions among the focus, principles, and commitments of each perspective.

The constructivist orientation focuses upon individuals reflecting on experience to make meaning of their worlds, often for the purpose of self-development and growth. Educators are advised to organize experiences for learning, coach and facilitate reflection, and help assess the meaning-making process.

The situative orientation suggests that educators can assist people to become fuller participants in a particular community by creating authentic conditions for people to experience and practice in, by arranging direct and indirect guidance for new-

comers to a community of practice, and by providing assistance
such as scaffolding in activities known as cognitive apprenticeship. Educators are encouraged to recognize how particular networks of action affect learning, and how spatial and temporal
geographies of a situation influence the networks of action.
Changes to the environment, tools, and opportunities for interaction in a community profoundly affect learning. Educators
can find pedagogical entry points in a community through recognizing possibilities for such changes and animating some action towards making them.

The psychoanalytic orientation suggests that educators
need to recognize the complex and largely unconscious dynamics of desire occurring at the heart of learning and teaching encounters. Rather than attempting to complete the desire for
knowledge, educators should assist people to dwell in and work
through the difficult psychic struggles of coming to face the self.
Finally, educators are encouraged to look carefully at their own
contradictory desires, attempting to understand their own unconscious longings, and to confront the difficult knowledges
they resist.

The critical cultural orientation urges educators to engage
people in critical examination of how power circulates through
their own communities, how it shapes their own sense of experience and how it names some knowledges and identities and
ignores or discriminates against others. Educators promote resistance to dominant norms, expose exploitation and silent
forms of control, and reveal how human identities and creative
potential are restricted or distorted in their experiences. Strategies emphasize involving people in critiquing those beliefs that
support an unjust, unfree system. Learning is enmeshed with
action towards personal liberation and building a more equitable,
sustainable, just, life-giving social order.

The ecological orientation based on complexity and enaction theories focuses educators' attention on the unfolding systems and subsystems of a learning community, including their
own implications in those systems. The embodiment of knowledge and the relationships among the elements of a system—
such as its subsystems (including individual actions), images,
language, space, trajectories of joint action and dialogue—are

significant. Learning is considered embedded in all aspects of the system, not just the minds of individual people. Educators can help unblock areas of the system that repress or distort activities of ongoing creative, adaptive learning. They can design learning occasions with organic structures, create open spaces for community dialogue, and amplify random events of disequilibrium that catalyse modification of the system.

In considering and implementing these suggestions we must not forget the basic challenges leveled by many critics at educators "using" human experience for learning: Are we attempting to manage experience? How do we presume to understand others' experience? Under what rationale do we insert ourselves into others' experience? To what ends, and for whose interests, ultimately? And, how do we understand our own implications in our work with others? Ultimately the responsibility falls to readers, to consider carefully just what they are attempting to do through educational practice, and why. The incorporation of these conceptual frames—reflection, participation, psychic interference, cultural politics, and ecological relationships—may open more life-giving possibilities for educative practice in experiential learning.

Experiential learning needs to be envisioned with broader perspectives than self-improvement, skill development, and productivity. Educators can make moral choices to be advocates and critics: critics of the reductionism and power relations subsuming human learning and development to mass consumption and control, and advocates for social reconstruction through learning in compassion and grace.

NOTES

1. Lavin (1997) studied women educational leaders' experiential learning. Rossi (1995) and Troyan (1996) examined nurses' informal learning. Olscheske (1999) analysed learning among biotechnology communities of practice. These are just a few examples of research positioned to enhance organizational performance through understanding workers' experiential learning processes.

REFERENCES

Adams, D., & Dixon, N. M. (1997). Action learning at digital equipment. In M. Pedler (Ed.), *Action learning in practice (3rd ed.)*. (pp. 122–131).

Albanese, M. A., & Mitchell, S. M. (1993). Problem-based learning: A review of literature on its outcomes and implementation issues. *Academic Medicine, 68*, 52–81.

Alheit, P. (1998). On a contradictory way to the 'learning society': A critical approach. *Studies in the Education of Adults, 31* (1), 66–82.

Allman, P. (2001). *Critical education against global capitalism: Karl Marx and revolutionary critical education*. Westport, CT; London: Bergin & Garvey.

Alvesson, M., & Willmott, H. (1996). *Making sense of management: A critical introduction*. London: Sage.

Anderson, J. R., Reder, L. M., & Simon, H. A. (1996). Situated learning and education. *Educational Researcher, 25* (4), 5–11.

Aronowitsch, E., & Craaford, C. (1995). Problem-based learning in psychotherapeutic training. *Psychoanalytic Psychotherapy, 9*, 139–40.

Bagdan, P. J. (1999). Relationships between learning styles, demographics, delivery methods, study times and test achievements of hospitality undergraduates. Unpublished doctoral dissertation, Kansas State University.

Ball, G. S. (1999). Building a sustainable future through transformation. *Futures, 31*, 251–270.

Baptiste, I. (2001). Educating lone wolves: Pedagogical implications of human capital theory. *Adult Education Quarterly, 51* (3), 184–201.

Bataille, G. (1988). *Inner experience* (trans. L. A. Boldt). New York: State University of New York Press.

Bateson, G. (1979). *Mind and nature: A necessary unity*. New York: E. P. Dutton.

Baumgartner, L., & Merriam, S. (2000). *Adult learning and development: Multicultural stories*. Malabar, FL: Krieger.

Beckett, D. (2001). Hot action at work: Understanding 'understanding' differently. In T. Fenwick (Ed.), *Socio-cultural understandings of workplace learning*. San Francisco: Jossey-Bass/Wiley.

Beckett, D., & Hager, P. (2000). Making judgments as the basis for workplace learning: Towards an epistemology of practice. *International Journal of Lifelong Education*, 19 (4), 300–311.

Begley, K. A. (2000). *Learning styles among a selected group of entrepreneurs: Implications for entrepreneurship programs at institutions of higher education in the United States*. Unpublished doctoral dissertation, Wilmington College, DE.

Billett, S. (2001). *Learning in the workplace: Strategies for effective practice*. Sydney: Allen & Unwin.

Bion, W. (1994). *Learning from experience*. Northvale, NJ: Jason Aronson.

Bligh, J. (1995). Problem-based learning in medicine: An introduction. *Postgraduate Medical Journal*, 71, (836), 323–6.

Boshier, R., & Harre, D. (2001). The Moeawatea process: Service learning with Kiwi attitude. *New Zealand Journal of Adult Learning*, 27 (2). Available online at *http://www.est.educ. ubc.ca/rboshier/Rbmoeawatea.html* (retrieved October 10, 2001).

Boud, D., & Miller, N. (1996). Animating learning from experience. In D. Boud & N. Miller (Eds.), *Working with experience* (pp. 3–13). London: Routledge.

Boud, D., & Walker, D. (1991). *Experience and learning: Reflection at work*. Geelong, Victoria: Deakin University Press.

Boud, D., Keogh, R., & Walker, D. (1996). Promoting reflection in learning: A model. In R. Edwards, A. Hanson, & P. Raggatt (Eds.), *Boundaries of adult learning*. New York: Routledge.

Bowerman, J., & Peters, J. (1999). Design and evaluation of an action learning program. *Journal of Workplace Learning: Employee Counselling Today*, 11 (4), 131–139.

Boyle, D. P., Nackerud, L., & Kilpatrick, A. (1999). The road less traveled: Cross-cultural, international experiential learning. *International Social Work*, 42 (2), 201–14.

Bracher, M. (1993). *Lacan, discourse, and social change: A psychoanalytic cultural criticism*. Ithaca: Cornell University Press.

Bracher, M. (1999). Psychoanalysis and education. *Journal for the Psychoanalysis of Culture and Society*, 4 (2), 127–192.

Brandt, B. L., Farmer, J. A. Jr., & Buckmaster, A. (1993). Cognitive apprenticeship approach to helping adults learning. In D. Flannery, (Ed.), *Applying cognitive learning theory to adult learning* (pp. 69–78). San Francisco: Jossey-Bass.

Briton, D. (1997). Psychoanalysis and pedagogy as living practices. In T. R. Carson & D. Sumara (Eds.), *Action research as living practice* (pp. 45–63). New York: Peter Lang Publishing.

Britzman, D. P. (1998a). *Lost subjects, contested objects: Toward a psychoanalytic inquiry of learning*. New York: State University of New York Press.

Britzman, D. P. (1998b). Some observations on the working of learning. *JCT Journal of Curriculum Theorizing, 14* (2), 53–59.

Brookfield, S. D. (1987). *Developing critical thinkers: Challenging adults to explore alternative ways of thinking and acting*. San Francisco: Jossey Bass.

Brookfield, S. D. (1993). Through the lens of learning: How the visceral experience of learning reframes teaching. In D. Boud, C. Cohen, & D. Walker (Eds.), *Using experience for learning* (pp. 21–31). Buckingham, UK: Society for Research into Higher Education and Open University Press.

Brookfield, S. D. (1995). *Becoming a critically reflective teacher*. San Francisco: Jossey Bass.

Brookfield, S. D. (2001). Repositioning ideology critique in a critical theory of adult education. *Adult Education Quarterly, 52* (9), 7–22.

Brookfield, S. D. (2002a). Reassessing subjectivity, criticality, and inclusivity: Marcuse's challenge to adult education. *Adult Education Quarterly, 52* (4), 265–280.

Brookfield, S. D. (2002b). Overcoming alienation as the practice of adult education: The contribution of Erich Fromm to a critical theory of adult learning and education. *Adult Education Quarterly, 52* (2), 96–111.

Brown, J. S., & Duguid, P. (1993). Stolen knowledge. *Educational Technology*, 10–15.

Brown, J. S., Collins, A., & Duguid, P. (1989). Situated cognition and the culture of learning. *Educational Researcher, 18* (1), 32–42.

Caffarella, R. S., & Olson, S. K. (1993). Psycho-social development of women: A critical review of the literature. *Adult Education Quarterly, 43* (3), 125–151.

Caffarella, R. S., Barnett, S., & Bruce, G. (1994). Characteristics of adult learners and foundations of experiential learning. *New Directions in Adult and Continuing Education*, no. 62, 29–42.

Capra, F. (1996). *The web of life: A new scientific understanding of living systems*. New York: Anchor Books.

Casey, M. B., & Howson, P. (1993). Educating pre-service students based on a problem-centered approach to teaching. *Journal of Teacher Education, 44* (5), 361–369.

Castellano, M. B. (2000). Updating aboriginal traditions of knowledge. In G. J. S. Dei, B. L. Hall, & D. G. Rosenberg (Eds.), *Indigenous knowledges in global contexts* (pp. 21–36).Toronto: University of Toronto Press.

Casti, J. L. (1994). *Complexification: Explaining a paradoxical world through the science of surprise*. New York: HarperCollins.

Chapman, V-L. (1996). *"All this talk!" Stories of women learning*. Unpublished master's thesis, University of British Columbia, Vancouver, BC.

Clandinin, D. J., & Connelly, M. (1995). *Teachers' professional knowledge landscapes*. New York: Teachers College Press.

Clark, M. C., & Dirkx, J. M. (2000). Moving beyond a unitary self: A reflective dialogue. In A. Wilson & E. Hayes (Eds.), *Handbook of adult and continuing education*. San Francisco: Jossey Bass.

Clark, M. C., & Wilson, A. (1991). Context and rationality in Mezirow's theory of transformational learning. *Adult Education Quarterly, 41* (2), 75–91.

Clover, D. E., Follen, S., & Hall, B. (2000). *The nature of transformation: Environmental adult education* (2nd ed.). Toronto: Ontario Institute for Studies in Education/University of Toronto.

Cognition and Technology Group at Vanderbilt. (1990). Anchored instruction and its relation to situated cognition. *Educational Researcher, 19* (6), 2–10.

Collins, M. (1991). *Adult education as vocation*. New York and London: Routledge.

Collins, P. H. (1990). *Black feminist thought: Knowledge, consciousness, and the politics of empowerment*. New York: Routledge.

Colliver, J. A. (2000). Effectiveness of problem-based learning curricula. *Academic Medicine, 75,* 259–266.

Cook, S. D. N., & Yanow, D. (1993). Culture and organizational learning. *Journal of Management Inquiry, 2* (4), 373–390.

Coover, C., Deacon, E., Esser, C., & Moore, C. (1993). *Resource manual for a living revolution*. Gabriola Island, BC: New Society Publishers.

Cope, B., & Kalantzis, M. (2000). *Multiliteracies: Literacy learning and the design of social futures*. London and New York: Routledge.

Cranton, P. (1996). *Professional development as transformative learning*. San Francisco: Jossey-Bass.

Cunningham, P. (1993). The politics of workers' education: Preparing workers to sleep with the enemy. *Adult Learning, 5* (1), 13–17.

Daloz, L. A. (1999). *Mentor*. San Francisco: Jossey-Bass.

Davis, B., & Sumara, D. J. (1997). Cognition, complexity and teacher education. *Harvard Educational Review, 67* (1), 105–125.

Davis, B., Sumara, D. J., & Luce-Kapler, R. (2000). *Engaging minds: Learning and teaching in a complex world.* Mahwah, NJ: Erlbaum.

Delli-Carpini, M., & Keeter, S. (2000). What should be learned through service learning? *Political Science and Politics, 33* (3), 635–37.

Deshler, D. (1990). Metaphor analysis: Exorcising social ghosts. In J. Mezirow & Associates (Eds.), *Fostering critical reflection in adulthood: A guide to transformative and emancipatory learning* (pp. 296–313). San Francisco: Jossey-Bass.

Dewey, J. (1938). *Experience and education.* New York: Collier Books.

Dilworth, R. L., & Willis, V. J. (2003). *Action learning: Images and pathways.* Malabar, FL: Krieger.

Doll, W. Jr. (1993). *A post-modern perspective on curriculum.* New York: Teachers College Press.

Dominicé, P. (2000). *Learning from our lives: Using educational biographies with adults.* San Francisco: Jossey-Bass/Wiley.

Easton, P. (2000). *Learning in the community.* Tallahassee, FL: Florida State University, Adult and Continuing Education. Available online at *http://www.fsu.edu/!adult-ed/courses/ADE4930.html* (retrieved October 15, 2001).

Edwards, R. (1994). Are you experienced? Postmodernity and experiential learning. *International Journal of Lifelong Education, 13* (6), 423–439.

Edwards, R. (1998). Flexibility, reflexivity and reflection in the contemporary workplace. *International Journal of Lifelong Education, 17* (6), 377–388.

Edwards, R., & Usher, R. (2000). *Globalisation and pedagogy: Space, place and identity.* London, Routledge.

Ellsworth, E. (1992). Why doesn't this feel empowering? Working through the repressive myths of critical pedagogy. In C. Luke & J. Gore (Eds.), *Feminisms and critical pedagogy* (pp. 90–119). New York: Routledge.

Ellsworth, E. (1997). *Teaching positions: Difference, pedagogy, and the power of address.* New York: Teachers College Press.

ELP (2000). The experiential learning program in evidence-based practice for health professionals: Program overview. Available online at *http://www.cche.net/elp/news/ELPoverview.htm* (retrieved November 30, 2001).

Eraut, M. (2000). Non-formal learning, implicit learning and tacit knowledge in professional work. In F. Coffield (Ed.), *The necessity of informal learning: The learning society* (pp. 12–31). Bristol: The Policy Press.

Eyler, J., & Giles, D. E. (1999). *Where's the learning in service learning?* San Francisco: Jossey-Bass/Wiley.

Felman, S. (1987). *Jacques Lacan and the adventure of insight: Psychoanalysis in contemporary culture.* Cambridge, MA: Harvard University Press.

Fenwick, T. (1997). Questioning the learning organization concept. In S. M. Scott, B. Spencer, & A. Thomas (Eds.), *Learning for life: Readings in Canadian adult education* (pp. 140–152). Toronto: Thompson.

Fenwick, T. (2001). Work knowing on the fly: Post-corporate enterprise cultures and co-emergent epistemology. *Studies in Continuing Education, 23* (1), 243–259.

Fenwick, T., & Parsons, J. (1998). Boldly solving the world: Problem-based learning in professional education. *Studies in the Education of Adults, 30* (1), 53–66.

Field, J. (2000). *Lifelong learning and the new educational order.* Stoke-on-Trent, Staffordshire, UK and Sterling, VA: Trentham Books.

Finger, M., & Asún, J. (2001). *Adult education at the crossroads: Learning our way out.* London and New York: Zed Books.

Fisher, R. C. (1994). The potential for problem-based learning in pharmacy education: A clinical therapeutics course in diabetes. *American Journal of Pharmaceutical Education, 58* (2), 183–189.

Flannery, D. D. (2000). Connection. In E. Hayes & D. D. Flannery (Eds.), with A. K. Brooks, E. J. Tisdell, & J. M. Hugo, *Women as learners: The significance of gender in adult learning* (pp. 111–138). San Francisco: Jossey-Bass.

Foley, G. (1999). *Learning in social action: A contribution to understanding informal education.* London and New York: Zed Books.

Foucault, M. (1980). *Discipline and punish: The birth of the prison* (trans. A. Sheridan). New York: Vintage.

Foucault, M. (1988). Technologies of the self. In L. Martin, H. Gutman, & P. Hutton (Eds.), *Technologies of the self: A seminar with Michel Foucault* (pp. 16–49). Amherst: University of Massachusetts Press.

Fraser, W. (1995). *Learning from experience: Empowerment or incorporation?* Leicester, England and Wales: The National Organization for Adult Learning.

Freire, P. (1970). *Pedagogy of the oppressed.* (trans. Myra Bergman Tramos). New York: Seabury Press.

Garrick, J. (1999). The dominant discourses of learning at work. In D. Boud & J. Garrick (Eds.), *Understanding learning in work* (pp. 216–231). London: Routledge.

Garrick, J., & Usher, R. (2000). Flexible learning, contemporary work and enterprising selves. *Electronic Journal of Sociology.* Available online at *http://www.sociology.org/content/vol005.001/garrick-usher.html* (retrieved November 20, 2001).

Gass, M., & Gillis, (1995). Focusing on the "solution" rather than the "problem": Empowering client change through adventure experiences. *Journal of Experiential Education, 18* (2), 63–69.

Gilbert, J. (1998). Reading colorblindness: Negation as an engagement with social difference. *JCT: Journal of Curriculum Theorizing, 14* (2), 29–34.

Giroux, H. (1992). *Border crossings: Cultural workers and the politics of education.* London and New York: Routledge.

Giroux, H. (1996). *Counternarratives: Cultural studies and critical pedagogies in postmodern spaces.* New York: Routledge.

Giroux, H., & McLaren, P. (Eds.). (1994). *Between borders: Pedagogy and the politics of cultural studies.* New York: Routledge.

Gold, J., Watson, S., & Rix, M. (2000). Learning for change by telling stories. In J. McGoldrick, J. Stewart, & S. Watson (Eds.), *Understanding human resource development: A resource based approach.* London: Routledge.

Gore, J. (1993). *The struggle for pedagogies: Critical and feminist discourses as regimes of truth.* New York: Routledge.

Graveline, F. J. (1998). *Circle works: Transforming Eurocentric consciousness.* Halifax, NS: Fernwood.

Greeno, J. (1997). On claims that answer the wrong question. *Educational Researcher, 27* (1), 5–17.

Griffin, C. (1992). Absorbing experiential learning. In J. Mulligan & C. Griffin (Eds.), *Empowerment through experiential learning* (pp. 31–36). London: Kogan Page.

Grossman, J. (1999). Workers and knowledge. In *Proceedings of Researching Work and Learning, a First International Conference* (pp. 207–216). Leeds, UK: University of Leeds.

Grosz, E. (1994). *Volatile bodies: Toward a corporeal feminism.* Bloomington and Indianapolis: Indiana University Press.

Grumet, M. (1992). Existential and phenomenological foundations of autobiographical methods. In W. F. Pinar & W. M. Reynolds (Eds.), *Understanding the curriculum as phenomenological and deconstructed text* (pp. 28–43). New York: Teachers College Press.

Harris, J. (1999). Ways of seeing the recognition of prior learning (RPL): What contribution can such practices make to social inclusion? *Studies in the Education of Adults*, 20 (2).

Harris, J. (2000). *RPL: Power, pedagogy and possibility*. Pretoria: Human Sciences Research Council.

Harrison, R. (2000). Learner managed learning: Managing to learn or learning to manage? *International Journal of Lifelong Education, 19* (4), 312–321.

Hart, M. U. (1992). *Working and educating for life*. London: Routledge.

Hart, M. U. (1993). Educative or miseducative work: A critique of the current debate on work and education. *Canadian Journal for the Study of Adult Education, 7* (1), 19–36.

Hayes, E., Flannery, D., with Brooks, A. K., Tisdell, E. J., & Hugo, J. M. (2000). *Women as learners: The significance of gender in adult learning*. San Francisco: Jossey-Bass.

Heaney, T. (1996). *Adult education for social change: From center stage to the wings and back again*. ERIC Clearinghouse on Adult, Career and Vocational Education, Center on Education and Training for Employment, Information Series No. 365. Columbus, OH.

Heron, J. (1992). *Feeling and personhood: Psychology in another key*. London: Sage.

Herz, B., & Merz, W. (1998). Experiential learning and the effectiveness of economic simulation games. *Simulation & Gaming, 29* (2), 238–250.

Holst, J. (2002). *Social movements, civil society, and radical adult education*. New York: Routledge.

hooks, b. (1994). *Teaching to transgress: Education as the practice of freedom*. London: Routledge.

Horton, M. (1990). *The long haul*. New York: Doubleday.

Howard, J. (1993). *Praxis I, Faculty casebook on community service-learning*. Ann Arbor, MI: OCSL press.

Hull, C. (1992). Making experience count: Facilitating the APEL process. In J. Mulligan & C. Griffin (Eds.), *Empowerment through experiential learning: Explorations of good practice* (pp. 118–123). London: Kogan Page.

Jarvinen, A. (1998). The experiential learning approach. *Lifelong Learning in Europe, 3*, 132.

Jarvis, P. (1987). *Adult learning in the social context*. London: Croom Helm.

Kane, L. (2001). *Popular education and social change in Latin America*. Nottingham, UK: Russell Press,

Karpiak, I. (2000). Evolutionary theory and the new sciences. *Studies in Continuing Education, 22* (1), 29–44.

Kayes, D. C. (2001). *Experiential learning in teams: A study in learning style, group process and integrative complexity in ad hoc groups.* Unpublished doctoral dissertation, Case Western Reserve University, Cleveland, OH.

Keck, M. E., & Sikkink, K. (1998). *Activists beyond borders: Advocacy networks in international politics.* Ithaca: Cornell University Press.

Kellner, D. (1995). *Media culture.* London: Routledge.

Kelly, U. A. (1997). *Schooling desire: Literacy, cultural politics, and pedagogy.* New York: Routledge.

Kincheloe, J. L. (1999). *How do we tell the workers? The socioeconomic foundations of work and vocational education.* Boulder, CO: Westview Press.

Kinsley, C. W., & McPherson, K. (1995). *Enhancing the curriculum through service learning.* Alexandra, VA: Association for Supervision and Curriculum Development.

Klein, M. (1988). Notes on some schizoid mechanisms. In *Envy and gratitude and other works 1946–1963.* London: Virago Press [1946].

Knowles, M. S. (1970). *The modern practice of adult education: Andragogy vs. pedagogy.* New York: Cambridge Books.

Kolb, D. A. (1984). *Experiential learning.* Englewood Cliffs, NJ: Prentice-Hall.

Kolb, D. A. (1998). Experiential learning: From discourse model to conversation. Interview with David Kolb. *Lifelong Learning in Europe, 3*, 148–153.

Kolb, D. A., & Kolb, A. (2000). *Experiential learning bibliography.* Available online at *dak5@msn.com* (retrieved June 5, 2001).

Kolb, D. A., Boyatzis, R., & Mainemelis, C. (2001). Experiential learning theory: Previous research and new directions. In R. Sternberg & L. Zhang (Eds.), *Perspectives on cognitive learning, and thinking styles.* Mahwah, NJ: Erlbaum.

Lacan, J. (1978). *The four fundamental concepts of psycho-analysis* (trans. A. Sheridan). New York: Norton.

Lather, P. (1991). *Getting smart: Feminist research and pedagogy with/in the postmodern.* New York: Routledge.

Lather, P. (2000). Reading the image of Rigoberto Menchú: Undecidability and language lessons. *Qualitative Studies in Education, 13* (2), 153–162.

Latour, B. (1993). *We have never been modern.* Hemel Hempstead: Harvester Wheatsheaf.

Lave, J. (1988). *Cognition in practice: Mind, mathematics and culture in everyday life.* Cambridge, England: Cambridge University Press.

Lave, J., & Chaiklin, S. (1993). *Understanding practice: Perspectives in activity and context.* New York: Cambridge University Press.

Lave, J., & Wenger, E. (1991). *Situated learning: Legitimate peripheral participation.* New York: Cambridge Press.

Lavin, R. (1997). *Learning from experience: The professional practical knowledge of female educational leaders in Nebraska.* Unpublished doctoral dissertation, University of Nebraska, Lincoln, NE.

Leavy, B. (1998). The concept of learning in the strategy field. *Management Learning, 29* (4), 337–366.

Levitt, B., & March, J. G. (1988). Organizational learning. *Annual Review of Sociology, 14,* 319–340.

Lindeman, E. C. (1926). *The meaning of adult education.* New York: New Republic.

Linds, W. (2000). The spiraling journey(s) of a living/loving popular theatre. In P. Willis, R. Smith, & E. Collins (Eds.), *Being, seeking, telling: Expressive approaches to qualitative adult education research* (pp. 403–420). Queensland, Australia: Post Pressed.

Loutzenheiser, L. W. (2001). "If I teach about these issues they will burn down my house": The possibilities and tensions of queered, antiracist pedagogy. In K. K. Kumashiro (Ed.), *Troubling intersections of race and sexuality: Queer students of colour and anti-oppressive education* (pp. 195–214). Lanham, MD: Rowan & Littlefield.

Lovelock, J. (1979). *Gaia, a new look at life on earth.* New York: Oxford University Press.

MacKeracher, D. (1996). *Making sense of adult learning.* Toronto: Culture Concepts.

Malinen, A. (2000). *Adult experiential learning.* University of Jyvaskyla: SoPhi.

Mann, K. V., & Kaufman, D. M. (1995). A response to the ACME-TRI Report: The Dalhousie problem-based learning curriculum. *Medical Education, 29* (1), 13–21.

Marando, V. L., & Melchior, M. B. (1997). On site, not out of mind: The role of experiential learning in the political science doctoral program. *Political Science and Politics, 30* (4), 723–728.

Margetson, D. (1994). Current educational reform and the significance of problem-based learning. *Studies in Higher Education, 19* (1), 5–20.

Marquardt, M. J. (1999). *Action learning in action: Transforming problems and people for world-class organizational learning.* London: Davies-Black.

Marsick, V., & O'Neil, J. (1999). The many faces of action learning. *Management Learning, 30* (2), 159–176.

Marsick, V., & Watkins, K. E. (1992). Towards a theory of informal and incidental learning in organizations. *International Journal of Lifelong Education, 11* (4), 287–300.

Maturana, H., & Varela, F. (1987). *The tree of knowledge: The biological roots of human understanding.* Boston: Shambhala.

McIsaac, E. (2000). Oral narratives as a site of resistance: Indigenous knowledge, colonialism, and western discourse. In G. J. S. Dei, B. L. Hall, & D. G. Rosenberg (Eds.), *Indigenous knowledges in global contexts* (pp. 89–101). Toronto: University of Toronto Press.

McLaren, P. (1989). *Life in schools: An introduction to critical pedagogy in the foundations of education.* New York: Longman.

Melamed, L. (1987). The role of play in adult learning. In D. Boud & V. Griffin (Eds.), *Appreciating adults learning* (pp. 13–24). London: Kogan Page.

Merriam, S. B., & Caffarella, R. (1999). *Learning in adulthood: A comprehensive guide.* San Francisco: Jossey-Bass.

Merriam, S. B., & Heuer, B. (1996). Meaning-making, adult learning, and development: A model with implications for practice. *International Journal of Lifelong Education, 15* (4), 243–255.

Mezirow, J. (1990). How critical reflection triggers transformative learning. In J. Mezirow & Associates (Eds.), *Fostering critical reflection in adulthood: A guide to transformative and emancipatory learning* (pp. 1–20). San Francisco: Jossey-Bass.

Mezirow, J. (1991). *Transformative dimensions of adult learning.* San Francisco: Jossey-Bass.

Mezirow, J. (1996). Contemporary paradigms of learning. *Adult Education Quarterly, 46* (3), 158–173.

Mezirow, J., & Associates (Eds.). (2000). *Learning as transformation: Critical perspectives on a theory in practice.* San Francisco: Jossey Bass.

Michelson, E. (1996). Usual suspects: Experience, reflection, and the (en)gendering of knowledge. *International Journal of Lifelong Education, 15* (6), 438–454.

Michelson, E. (1999). Carnival, paranoia, and experiential learning. *Studies in the Education of Adults, 31* (2), 140–154.

Miller, N. (2000). Learning from experience in adult education. In A. Wilson & E. Hayes (Eds.), *Handbook of adult and continuing education* (pp. 71–86). San Francisco: Jossey-Bass.

Mojab, S. (2001). New resources for revolutionary critical education. *Convergence, 34* (1), 118–125.

Moliterno, J. E. (1995). Professional preparedness: A comparative study of law graduates' perceived readiness for professional ethics issues. *Law and Contemporary Problems, 58,* 259–86.

Newman, J. (1991). *Interwoven conversations: Learning and teaching through critical reflection.* Toronto: Ontario Institute for Studies in Education.

Newman, J. (1998). *Tensions of teaching: Beyond tips to critical reflection.* New York and London: Teachers College Press; Canada: Canadian Scholars' Press.

Newman, M. (1999). *Maeler's regard: Images of adult learning.* Sydney, Australia: Stewart Victor Publishing.

Newstrom, J. W., & Scannell, E. E. (1980). *Games trainers play: Experimental learning exercises.* New York: McGraw-Hill.

Nonaka, I., & Takeuchi, H. (1995). *The knowledge-creating company.* Oxford: Oxford University Press.

Nussbaumer, L. L. (1998). *The relationship between learning styles and visualization skills among interior design students.* Unpublished doctoral dissertation, University of Minnesota, Minneapolis-St. Paul, MN.

O'Brien, S. L. (2000). *Registered nurse's learning styles and accuracy in interpretation of ECG rhythms.* Unpublished doctoral dissertation. Eastern Michigan University, Ypsilanti, MI.

Olscheske, T. (1999). *Knowledge creation and discovery learning teams: A case study exploring the dynamics of knowledge creation, utilization and transfer in biotechnology R&D groups.* Unpublished doctoral dissertation, University of Wisconsin, Madison, WI.

Orner, M. (1992). Interrupting the calls for student voice in liberatory education: A feminist poststructuralist perspective. In C. Luke & J. Gore (Eds.), *Feminisms and critical pedagogy* (pp. 74–89). New York: Routledge.

Owen, H. (1997). *Open space technology: A user's guide.* San Francisco: Berrett-Koehler.

Parker, M., & Slaughter, J. (1994). *Working smart: A union guide to participation programs and reengineering.* Detroit MI: Labor Notes.

Parks Daloz, L. A., Keen, C. H., Keen, J. P., & Daloz Parks, S. D. (1996). *Common fire: Lives of commitment in a complex world.* Boston: Beacon Press.

Philips, D. C. (1995). The good, the bad, and the ugly: The many faces of constructivism. *Educational Researcher, 24* (7), 5–12.

Piaget, J. (1966). *The psychology of intelligence.* Totowa, NJ: Littlefield, Adams, and Co.

Pile, S., & Thrift, N. (1995). Mapping the subject. In S. Pile & N.

Thrift (Eds.), *Mapping the subject: Geographies of cultural transformation* (pp. 13–51). London: Routledge.

Pimentel, J. R. (1999). Design of net-learning systems based on experiential learning. *Journal of Asynchronous Learning Networks, 3* (2). Available online at *http://www.aln.org/alnweb/journal/Vol3_*issue2/pimentel.htm (retrieved November 30, 2001).

Plexus Institute. (2000). *Edgeware applications.* Available online at *http://www.plexusinstitute. com/edgeware/archive/think/main_*app-h.html (retrieved July 5, 2001).

Postle, D. (1993). Putting the heart back into learning. In D. Boud, R. Cohen, & D. Walker (Eds.), *Using experience for learning* (pp. 33–45). Buckingham: Society for Research into Higher Education & Open University Press.

Prawat, R. S. (1993). The value of ideas: Problems versus possibilities in learning. *Educational Researcher,* (August-September 1993), 5–16.

Prentki, T., & Selman, J. (2000). *Popular theatre in political culture.* Bristol, UK: Intellect Books.

Priest, S., & Gass, M. (1997). An examination of "problem-solving" versus "solution-focused" facilitation styles in a corporate setting. *Journal of Experiential Education, 20* (1), 34–39.

Prigogine, I. (1997). *The end of certainty: Time, chaos, and the new laws of nature.* New York: The Free Press.

Probert, B. (1999). Gendered workers and gendered work: Implications for women's learning. In D. Boud & J. Garrick (Eds.), *Understanding learning in work* (pp. 98–116). London: Routledge.

Reeve, F., & Gallacher, J. (1999). How are the discourses of work-based learning influencing practices? In *Proceedings of Researching Work and Learning, a First International Conference* (pp. 124–130). Leeds, UK: University of Leeds.

Renner, P. (1994). *The art of teaching adults.* Vancouver, BC: Training Associates.

Revans, R. (1980). *Action learning: New techniques for management.* London: Blond and Briggs.

Richards, A. (1992). Adventure-based experiential learning. In J. Mulligan & C. Griffin (Eds.), *Empowerment through experiential learning* (pp. 155–162). London: Kogan Page.

Rogoff, B. (1990). *Apprenticeship in thinking: Cognitive development in social context.* New York: Oxford University Press.

Rose, M. (1999). "Our hands will know": The development of tactile diagnostic skill—Teaching, learning and situated cognition in a physical therapy program. *Anthropology and Education Quarterly,* *30* (2), 133–160.

Rossi, L. (1995). *How nurses gain clinical expertise through informal learning in the workplace.* Unpublished doctoral dissertation, Columbia University Teachers College, New York.

Saavedra, E. (1996). Teachers' study groups: Contexts for transformative learning and action. *Theory into Practice, 35,* 271–277.

Saddington, T. (1998). Exploring the roots and branches of experiential learning. *Lifelong Learning in Europe,* 3, 133–138.

Salomon, G., & Perkins, D. N. (1998). Individual and social aspects of learning. In P. D. Pearson & A. Iran-Nejad (Eds.), *Review of Research in Education, 23,* 1–24.

Salt, B., Cervero, R., & Herod, A. (2000). Workers' education and neoliberal globalization: An adequate response to transnational corporations? *Adult Education Quarterly, 51* (1), 9–31.

Saltman, K. (1998). Why doesn't this feel political? *The Journal of Critical Pedagogy.* Available online at *http://www.lib.wmc.edu/pub/ jcp/issuell-1/saltman.html* (retrieved October 28, 2000).

Sawada, D. (1991). Deconstructing reflection. *The Alberta Journal of Educational Research, 37* (4), 349–366.

Schied, F. M. (1995). How did humans become resources anyway? HRD and the politics of learning in the workplace. In S. Scott (Ed.), *Proceedings of the 26th Annual Adult Education Research Conference* (pp. 287–292). Edmonton, AB: University of Alberta.

Schön, D. A. (1983). *The reflective practitioner.* New York: Basic Books.

Schön, D. A. (1987). *Educating the reflective practitioner.* New York: Basic Books.

Senge, P. (1999). *The dance of change: The challenges to sustaining momentum in learning organizations.* New York: Currency/Doubleday.

Senge, P., Kleiner, A., Roberts, C., Ross, R., & Smith, B. (1994). *The fifth discipline fieldbook: Strategies and tools for building a learning organization.* New York: Doubleday.

Sfard, A. (1998). On two metaphors for learning and the dangers of choosing just one. *Educational Researcher, 27* (2), 4–13.

Siens, C. M., & Ebmeier, H. (1996). Developmental supervision and the reflective thinking of teachers. *Journal of Curriculum and Supervision, 11* (4), 299–319.

Silverman, K. (1992). *Male subjectivity at the margins.* New York: Routledge, Chapman and Hall.

Simon, R. I., Dippo, D., & Schenke, A. (1991). *Learning work: A critical pedagogy of work education.* Toronto: OISE Press.

Solomon, N. (2001). Workplace learning as cultural technology. In T. Fenwick (Ed.), *Sociocultural perspectives on learning through work* (pp. 41–52). San Francisco: Jossey Bass.

Spolin, V. (1963). *Improvisation for the theatre.* Evanston, IL: Northwest University Press.

Stewart, I. (1997). *Intellectual capital: The new wealth of organizations.* New York: Doubleday.

Sumara, D., & Davis, B. (1997). Enlarging the space of the possible: Complexity, complicity, and action research practices. In D. Sumara & T. Carson (Eds.), *Action research as a living practice* (pp. 299–312). New York: Peter Lang.

Taylor, E. W. (1998). *The theory and practice of transformative learning: A critical review* (information series no. 374). Columbus, OH: ERIC Clearinghouse on Adult, Career and Vocational Education, Center on Education and Training for Employment.

Taylor, E. W. (2001). Transformative learning theory: A neurobiological perspective of the role of emotions and unconscious ways of knowing. *International Journal of Lifelong Education, 20* (3), 218–236.

Tisdell, E. J. (1995). *Creating inclusive environments: Insights from multicultural education and feminist pedagogy* (information series no. 361). Columbus, OH: ERIC Clearinghouse on Adult, Career and Vocational Education, Center on Education and Training for Employment.

Tisdell, E. J. (1998). Poststructural feminist pedagogies: The possibilities and limitations of feminist emancipatory adult learning theory and practice. *Adult Education Quarterly, 48* (3), 139–156.

Tobias, R. (1999). Lifelong learning under a comprehensive national qualifications framework: Rhetoric and reality. *International Journal of Lifelong Education, 18* (2), 110–118.

Todd, S. (Ed.). (1997). *Learning desire: Perspectives on pedagogy, culture, and the unsaid.* New York and London: Routledge.

Townley, B. (1994). *Reframing human resource management: Power, ethics, and the subject at work.* London: Sage.

Troyan, P. (1996). *How nurses learn about management through informal learning in the workplace.* Unpublished doctoral dissertation, Columbia University Teachers College, New York.

Usher, R., & Edwards, R. (1995). Confessing all? A 'postmodern' guide to the guidance and counseling of adult learners. *Studies in the Education of Adults, 27* (1), 9–23.

Usher, R., & Solomon, N. (1999). Experiential learning and the shaping of subjectivity in the workplace. *Studies in the Education of Adults, 31* (2), 155–163.

Usher, R., Bryant, I., & Johnston, R. (1997). *Adult education and the postmodern challenge: Learning beyond the limits.* New York: Routledge.

Vandenabeele, J., & Wildemeersch, D. (2000). Learning for sustainable development: Examining life world transformation among farmers. In D. Wildemeersch, M. Finger, & T. Jansen (Eds.), *Adult education and social responsibility* (2nd ed.) (pp. 117–133). New York: Peter Lang.

Vandenberg, D. (1999). Review of teaching positions: Difference, pedagogy and the power of address by Elizabeth Ellsworth. *Educational Studies, 30* (1), 74–79.

Varela, J. (1989). Laying down a path while walking. In W. E. Thompson (Ed.), *Gaia* (pp. 48–63). Cambridge, MA: Shambhala.

Varela, F. J, Thompson, E., & Rosch, E. (1991). *The embodied mind: Cognitive science and human experience.* Cambridge, MA: MIT Press.

Von Bertalanffy, L. (1971). *General system theory: Foundations, development, applications.* London: Allen Lane.

Von Glaserfeld, E. (1984). An introduction to radical constructivism. In P. Watzlawick (Ed.), *The invented reality* (pp. 17–40). New York: W. W. Norton.

Von Kotze, A. (2000). Adult education and training in the framework of reconstruction and development in South Africa. In D. Wildemeersch, M. Finger, & T. Jansen (Eds.), *Adult education and social responsibility* (2nd ed.) (pp. 153–176). New York: Peter Lang.

Vygotsky, L. S. (1978). *Mind in society: The development of higher psychological processes.* Cambridge, MA: Harvard University Press.

Waldrop, M. M. (1992). *Complexity: The emerging science at the edge of order and chaos.* New York: Simon and Schuster.

Walton, H. J., & Matthews, M. B. (1989). Essentials of problem-based learning. *Medical Education, 23,* 542–558.

Warner Weil, S., & McGill, I. (Eds.). (1989). *Making sense of experiential learning: Diversity in theory and practice.* London: Society for Research into Higher Education and Open University Press, Milton Keynes.

Weisbord, M., & Janoff, S. (1995). *Future search: An action guide to finding common ground in organizations and communities.* San Francisco: Berrett-Koehler.

Wells, G. (1995). Language and the inquiry-oriented curriculum. *Curriculum Inquiry, 25* (3), 233–248.

Welton, M. R. (1995). (Ed.) *In defense of the lifeworld: Critical per-*

spectives on adult learning. Albany: State University of New York Press.

Wenger, E. (1998). *Communities of practice: Learning, meaning and identity.* Cambridge: Cambridge University Press.

West, L. (1996). *Beyond fragments: Adults, motivation, and higher education—a biographical analysis.* London: Taylor and Francis.

West, L. (2001). *Doctors on the edge: General practitioners, health and learning in the inner city.* London: Free Association Books.

Wheatley, M. (1994). *Leadership and the new science.* San Francisco: Berrett-Koehler.

Wildemeersch, D., Jansen, T., Vandenabeele, J., & Jans, M. (1998). Social learning: A new perspective on learning in participatory systems. *Studies in Continuing Education, 20* (2), 251–264.

Willis, P., Smith, R., & Collins, E. (Eds.). (2000). *Being, seeking, telling: Expressive approaches to qualitative adult education research.* Queensland, Australia: Post Pressed.

Wilson, B. G., & Myers, K. M. (1999). Situated cognition in theoretical and practical contexts. In D. Jonassen & S. Land (Eds.), *Theoretical foundations of learning environments.* Mahwah, NJ: Erlbaum.

Young, R. (1990). *White mythologies.* New York: Routledge.

Zachary, L. J. (2000). *The mentor's guide: Facilitating effective learning relationships.* San Francisco: Jossey-Bass.

Zizek, S. (1991). *Looking awry: An introduction to Jacques Lacan through popular culture.* Cambridge, MA: Massachusetts Institute of Technology.

INDEX